# Love Rewired

# LOVE REWIRED

## Using Your Brain To Mend Your Heart

# David Kavanagh

ORPEN PRESS

Published by
Orpen Press
13 Adelaide Road
Dublin 2
Ireland

email: info@orpenpress.com

www.orpenpress.com

1 3 5 7 9 10 8 6 4 2

Paperback ISBN 978-1-78605-005-2
ePub ISBN 978-1-78605-006-9
Kindle ISBN 978-1-78605-007-6
PDF ISBN 978-1-78605-008-3

Printed in Dublin by SPRINTprint Ltd.

*For Breige and Éabha*

# Contents

# Contents

# Contents

# Contents

# Contents

# ACKNOWLEDGEMENTS

I would like to thank my friend and business partner, Joanne, for her belief in me and steadfast support throughout the years. I also need to thank Amy Brann for her guidance and patience, as she helped me navigate the world of neuroscience.

Thanks also to my therapy clients whose bravery and courage have inspired me to follow my own dreams as they followed theirs. I would like to give a special thanks to the thousands of couples who allowed my Avalon team to prepare them for marriage.

To my circle of friends who are like family to me, and to my family who are like friends to me: thank you for always being there.

Special gratitude must be extended to Grainne Gormley and Ruth O'Donnell who have been my mentors for the last ten years. I would have been lost (on many occassions) without your guidance.

To my publishers who hounded me, I needed it, so thank you. To my editor who tried to fix every possible issue with this manuscript, most of which I never even knew existed, thank you, Fiona.

To the community of neuroscience thinkers and researchers that made this book possible, thank you for the incredible work you are doing. The future is very exciting thanks to you.

Special thanks to my great friends Ian Mulcahy and Anne Sexton for their creativity and attention to detail. Their enthusiasm and support for this project helped me during some very challenging times.

I offer my thanks to Sebastian Czajkowski and Philip Wall for their loyalty and friendship and, more importantly, for building the website to accompany this book.

Thank you also to Muriel Fraser for doing some of the research that made this book possible.

# Acknowledgements

My legal team, managed by Lauren Martin, has managed to keep me from saying anything that might get me in trouble, so thank you, Lauren.

And thank you, the reader, for making this project worthwhile.

Finally to Breige and Éabha, who rewired my brain more than I ever believed possible. You have my love, always.

# FOREWORD

Pause for a moment and consider: what's most important to you in this world?

For many of us, the answer will be 'our relationships with others'. The depth and quality of our connections to others has a huge impact on our happiness. From the 1960s to the 1990s, psychology and psychiatry observed human relationships from the outside. Today we're in the privileged position of having another lens through which to understand ourselves. Now we have incredible insights from neuroscience that give us the opportunity to reshape how we play the game of life.

You have the ability to live more fully through your relationships. That is why giving time, attention and energy to implementing the strategies contained within this book will be the greatest gift you can give yourself and those around you. The success of your tomorrow is closely linked to how you relate to people today.

*Love Rewired* explains complex theories using accessible language. It brings your most valuable asset to life and shows you how to use it to its full potential. Using your brain to mend your heart is the essence of this book. This is not your average self-help book. It's a game changer.

Amy Brann, author of *Make your Brain Work: How to Maximize Your Efficiency, Productivity and Effectiveness*

# Introduction

The futurologist Alvin Toffler made the following prediction in his book *Future Shock*:

> As human relationships grow more transient and modular, the pursuit of love becomes, if anything, more frenzied. As conventional marriage proves itself less and less capable of delivering on its promise of lifelong love, we can even anticipate open public acceptance of temporary marriages. Instead of wedding 'until death do us part', couples will enter into matrimony knowing from the first that the relationship is likely to be short-lived (Toffler, p. 231).

With marriage breakdown at an all-time high, and with trial marriages and even trial separations commonplace, Toffler has proved correct in this and many of his other predictions. What he couldn't possibly have predicted, however, but that challenges marriage more than anything else, was the Internet. With any amount of pornography, online gambling and illicit sex just a few clicks away, relationships are under more strain than ever before.

It's not just our love relationships that have suffered, but our family and work relationships too. Today we experience more stress and more time poverty than Toffler did in the 1970s.

As parents, we struggle to spend quality time with our children, free from distractions or the push from corporations to spend, spend, and spend.

# Introduction

In work, our employers make more demands on us than ever before. According to recent research, the majority of us working in the industrialised world check our work emails even on holidays. Thanks to smartphones, we can take the office with us everywhere we go. We appear to be always 'on'.

Thankfully, the technological developments of the last 30 years have also brought with them some significant improvements for the study of human relationships. Neuroscience or brain science is one such area. More advances have been made in this field in the last 20 years than in the previous five centuries combined.

Using hi-tech scanners we can now watch blood flowing to different parts of the human brain and make reasonable deductions about what it means. Brain science has radically changed our understanding of who we are.

Most psychotherapy and psychiatry courses teach us about behaviour, but only from the observer position. Inferences are drawn about what behaviour means. Now, thanks to fMRI scanners, we finally have the technology to see inside people's heads and get a better idea why we do what we do.

Functional magnetic resonance imaging (fMRI) machines measure the magnetic properties of red blood cells that carry oxygen around the brain. When our brain is performing a specific task, it sends more oxygen to that area. Oxygen and glucose combine together to give the brain the fuel it needs to function. The fMRI machine can pinpoint an area of the brain to the nearest millimetre. When a given area is in use, it will light up on the computer monitor, telling us which parts of the brain are performing which functions.

Some of the greatest discoveries in brain science weren't all that hi-tech. In 1921, the German pharmacologist Otto Loewi had a dream that changed how we understood the way messages were sent through the brain. His dream gave him details of an experiment he should perform on frogs' hearts. So he got up and set to work. Before his dream it was believed that these messages were electrical in nature. After he did the experiment from his dream, which involved stimulating the vagus nerve on two frogs' hearts, he discovered they were chemical. Other scientists built on this work and proved that all communication between nerves is chemical.

The history of brain science is a bit gruesome. It really begins with scientists working on the brains of soldiers killed on the battlefields of our two World Wars. In later times, scientists experimented with electricity on people with brain injuries; in some cases while they were still conscious.

The field of neuroscience is changing rapidly as new discoveries are made every year so there is a risk that some of the information given here may be out of date in a few short years. This is a risk I have to take. I have endeavoured to ensure that the strategies, tools and skills we explore here will be more permanent, despite any new directions that brain research may take.

One thing that never changes is the need for people to connect to each other in more meaningful ways. The intrusion of technology into our most intimate moments means that no matter where 'progress' takes us, couples may struggle to stay together.

Scientists believe there are more cells (called neurons) in the human brain than there are stars in the universe. This means your potential as a human being is immense. Yet it's hard to feel excited about such facts when an argument over housework has left you angry or resentful.

To begin our journey, we will bore deep into the layers of the brain to see how each part of the brain affects how we are, who we are and who we can become. From here we will explore the unique and important functions that brain parts such as our amygdala play in regulating our emotions and helping us to relate more effectively.

While the brain is quite complex, for our purposes I'm going to use pictures to help us remember its functions. You will meet your 'Gorilla', your 'Professor' and even your 'inner Sherlock'!

*Love Rewired* isn't all about anatomy. It's more than the sum of its parts. We will explore how our minds can be tricked, despite their incredible sophistication. Simple errors of judgement are common to us all and have profound implications for how we relate to our lovers.

'You're an amazing person. You're incredibly funny. You're clever and wise. You recognise a great book when you see one.' That was an example of 'priming'. Priming is a tool we can use to influence others merely by giving them something to read. You will learn more about priming throughout this book and how its subtle influence can help your relationship.

The social sciences have also revealed a great deal about the way we think and relate. Behavioural economists such as the Nobel Prize-winner Daniel Kahneman have shed light on some of the perplexing characteristics of modern thinking and decision-making. We will learn that our memories are not to be trusted and that when it comes to making decisions, we're not in control the way we like to think we are.

Relationships are tricky, but there are a number of core issues, which, if navigated well, can give us the satisfaction we long for. These include trust, communication, healthy sexuality and stress management. Brain science has important insights into each.

But, if like many people reading this book, you're not in a committed relationship, or perhaps you've just come through a break-up, you can still benefit from the world of brain science. Expect to learn how brain science can make you more popular with the opposite sex, can help you arrange the perfect date, and even make you better in bed!

There is also a website, www.loverewired.com, to complement this book. There you will find bonus content, my blog, videos and links to other helpful neuroscience articles.

My hope is that this book evolves as we evolve. I would love you to contribute to this book and create a community of brain-science converts who spread the word that understanding the brain is the next stage of our evolution.

I would love to hear your thoughts about our book. Anything you think I've missed, I will endeavour to write about at a later date and publish on the website. This is your book, as much as it is mine.

But for now, get comfy, take a deep breath, relax and enjoy. (Just primed you there, by the way: read on to discover more about what this means.)

# THE NEUROSCIENCE OF DATING

The Perils of Coaching

William James

The Halo Effect

## THE PERILS OF COACHING

My career really took off when I announced to the media that I was Ireland's first professional dating coach, whose job it was to find love for singletons everywhere. I was inundated with requests for interviews. Back then, in 2003, no one had heard of such a role. Surely that was just something 'the Americans' went in for; Irish people are too sensible for that, surely? Not really. I was very busy for many years to follow, even becoming the first Internet dating coach in the history of the state. But the life of a professional dating coach wasn't all plain sailing.

I once appeared on a late-night talk show to discuss dating with two other panellists. Everything was going well until the host asked when I thought women should pay for dinner. I said they should at least offer to pay by the second date. This was jeered by the audience, much to my embarrassment. The other panellist, Baz Ashmawy (he of *50 Ways To Kill Your Mammy* fame) said that the guy should pay for as long as the lady allowed him. The audience roared their approval. I sank into my chair hoping the floor would suddenly open up like a crater and let me slide right in.

It seemed my idea wasn't that popular.

On a different occasion I was invited onto a judging panel for another well-known chat show. My job was to read hundreds of entries for the 'most loving couple in Ireland' competition; the grand prize was worth ten thousand euro. Three couples were chosen to take part in a live competition on the show a few weeks later.

I was in the audience when the competition was taking place. It was a Mr and Mrs-type challenge. It was a tie between two of the couples, leading to a tiebreaker. The host asked the last contestant, a young man in his mid twenties, the final question and presented him with three answers. 'Did your fiancée say answer A, B or C?'

Just as the host, John, said the letter 'C', the woman shrugged her shoulders. Her fiancé said, 'It was C, John.' John said, 'Congratulations, you have just won the ten thousand euro grand prize!'

The audience were stunned. Some applauded, many didn't. There was an uncomfortable atmosphere for the remainder of the show.

I was asked back by the producers a few days later to review the video footage of the competition, to see if there had been any funny business. I replayed over and over again the exact moment the woman had shrugged her shoulders. I looked carefully at her face to see if I could discern any micro-gestures – fleeting facial movements that show our true feelings. It became apparent that when she shrugged her shoulders, she smiled and grimaced at the same time. This indicated to me that she knew she was communicating with her fiancé through subterfuge. Who said romance is dead?

Perhaps their love for each other was just so strong they were prepared to do anything to prove it? They could have just entered the world's longest kissing competition, like Akekachai Tiranarat and his wife Raksana Taranarat. They entered, and won, this competition in 2011 by kissing each other for a staggering 46 hours, 24 minutes and 9 seconds. What a duo!

## WHY WE KISS

Kissing is the means by which we discover if our beloved has the right genes. The right genes for what, I hear you ask. Why to make babies, of course. We have a group of genes called the MHC, or major histocompatibility complex, which gives us our natural scent and taste. When we kiss someone, our brains are programmed to only find attractive those individuals who have opposite genes to us. This guarantees that any offspring that result from the union will have the best chance of survival. And you thought it was about romance, didn't you?

## What happens in our brains when we kiss?

During a kiss, the brain releases three chemicals: dopamine, oxytocin and serotonin. The combination of all three together gives us a natural high, similar to what is produced by heroin or cocaine. But kissing is much cheaper and safer. No wonder the Thai couple lasted 46 hours!

## What about hugs?

Hugs have the following core benefits.

- Hugs reduce our fear of mortality. Studies have shown that existential angst can be eased through touch.
- Hugs release oxytocin. Oxytocin has been proven to act on the brain's reward centre and give relief from stress.
- Hugs promote social bonding. When people hug, they trust each other more.
- The skin contains tiny cells called pacinian corpuscles that can sense touch, and that are in contact with the brain through the vagus nerve. These send messages to the brain to release chemicals like dopamine and serotonin during a hug, thus reducing tension and worry.

So whether you're dating, or in a long-term relationship, do yourself a favour and practise kissing with your partner, then finish off the session with a good, long, meaningful hug. Alternatively, if your lover needs a bit of cheering up, you could just hand them a pen.

## WILLIAM JAMES

No, the pen isn't so they can write you a love letter, the pen is to place between their teeth. They should keep the pen in position for 10 to 15 seconds at least. Why? I hear you ask. To explain, I need to introduce you to an important psychologist called William James.

William James was born in 1842, in New York. Brother of the novelist Henry James, William had a privileged upbringing, meeting some of the most influential people of the age. He studied medicine with the original aim of becoming a physician but a combination of factors put paid to that idea. James was fascinated by the human mind and created the very first psychology course in America. He observed: 'I originally studied medicine in order to be a physiologist, but I drifted into psychology and philosophy from a sort of fatality. I never had any philosophic instruction, the first lecture on psychology I ever heard being the first I ever gave.'

James began to research the relationship between emotions and behaviour. The accepted wisdom at the time was that if you got a sudden, unexpected shock, this would cause you to feel afraid. Then you would act afraid as a result. If you managed to get a promotion in your job, this would cause you to feel happy, so you would behave as though you were happy. In other words, events cause feelings, and feelings cause our behaviours.

James challenged this idea. He read about some experiments that Charles Darwin had been performing, which were aimed at recognising people's emotions by looking at photographs. James found it easy to judge what someone was feeling just by looking at their face. He could easily tell if someone was anxious or joyful. James wondered if by looking in a mirror and observing your own expressions you would then be able to tell what you were feeling. As James said himself, 'You do not run from a bear because you are afraid of it, but rather become afraid of the bear because you run from it.'

What James argued was that perhaps the brain reacts before 'you' do, and eventually you observe what your brain has signalled your body to do, and from that observation you decide what you're feeling. This was a radical concept at the time.

Eventually his idea stuck. Today it's one of the most important concepts in the self-help field, known as acting 'as if'. It goes something like this: if I'm anxious before I go on a date, I need to act as someone who's confident. I should stand up straight, I should wear expensive, well-fitting clothing, and I should imagine myself being filled with confidence. This acting 'as if' will then cause my behaviour to change, and when I observe my new behaviour, I will conclude that I am indeed confident.

Whether you're single, dating or in a long-term relationship, the 'as if' principle has profound implications. Singletons who lack confidence need simply imagine what 'sexy' feels like and that experience can be theirs. Those of us who are dating can act 'as if' our lovers are crazy about us, and this will help us induce that feeling in them. Couples in crisis can imagine what life would be like if they were happy, and their new behaviours will trick them into thinking they are.

Okay, back to the pen question. Try it for yourself. Place a pen in between your teeth for 15 seconds and observe yourself 'smile' in a mirror. Your brain will now 'see' that you are smiling, conclude from this that you are happy, and thus release chemicals into your brain to make sure you *are* happy. William James observed that 'We don't laugh because we're happy, we're happy because we laugh.'

Gazing also has its own magical properties.

When we gaze into someone's eyes (a lover's eyes and not the stranger opposite you on the train), it releases a chemical called PEA (phenylethlamine). This makes us feel happy and content. Ideally the gazing has to be reciprocal or otherwise it's called staring, and that's just weird. Dr Eckhard Hess coined the term 'pupillometrics' in the 1960s to define the behaviours he observed in pupil dilation when he showed subjects photographs of different objects, including faces of attractive people.

Essentially, our pupils dilate when we see something or someone attractive. Next time you meet an attractive man or woman, look quickly to see if their pupils widened when your eyes locked. If they did, bingo, you've pulled!

## Can Fear Cause Lust?

Arthur Aron and his colleague Donald Dutton are two psychologists who have studied the impact of fear on levels of attraction. They organised an experiment that used two different bridges over the Capilano River in British Columbia. Men were approached by a research assistant posing as a market researcher either on one of the bridges that was swaying dangerously or on a different bridge that was far more secure.

The swaying bridge caused the men's heart rates to increase, due to fear. But the men believed that what they felt was passion for the researcher, and not fear. The men on the safer bridge had no such reaction. After they crossed the bridge, the researcher gave all the men her number on the pretext that she wanted to hear about their experience later, if they had anything they wanted to share with her. The vast majority of men who had used the dangerous bridge called her that evening. She didn't hear from the men who used the safer bridge.

The moral of the story is that fear generates lust. To increase the sexual chemistry between you and your date, just scare the pants off them, literally.

Alternatively you could just bring your date to a pitch-black room and see what happens next. Kenneth Gergen did exactly that. Gergen wanted to explore what happens to couples when they are left alone in the dark. He brought a number of people to a specially designed room fitted with infrared cameras that recorded in the dark. He found that strangers touched and hugged each other much more than they did when the lights were on. This experiment was eventually made into a popular TV show called *Dating in the Dark*.

In that programme another myth was exposed: that women don't judge men on looks. In fact, many of the female participants that were left alone with their date touched his face, caressed his arm and embraced him as the date was ending. They usually told the other female participants (who they could see) that they loved the sound of his voice and couldn't wait to see what he looked like when the lights came on. In reality, once the lights were turned on and she could see him clearly, it was fascinating how many women refused to meet the men they had previously been hugging, or in some cases kissing. Looks *were* everything, it seems.

Once you manage to survive any 'dating in the dark' experiences, the sure-fire way to make someone fall in love with you is to organise for them to do something very silly with you. Arthur Aron worked with a different colleague, this time a psychologist called Barbara Fraley, on the impact that silly behaviour had on a couple's experience of closeness. They split couples into two groups. One group was forced to learn a dance while playing silly games, the other couples were told just to learn the dance routine. After the routine was learned by both sets of couples, the couples were asked to rate how close they felt to one another. In every case the couples who had played the games rated themselves far closer than the couples who hadn't. The moral here is that by acting child-like and carefree, we can make ourselves feel closer as a couple. The good news is that acting silly together won't cost you a penny. Hallmark, eat your heart out.

Or then there's music. Mihaly Csikszentmihalyi wrote an interesting book about 'flow', otherwise known as the 'optimal state', where one is experiencing nothing but happiness from an activity, no matter how challenging the activity might be. When couples lose themselves in music, be it ballroom, samba or techno, they also lose inhibitions, and the endorphin rush they experience can really bring them closer. Or as Csikszentmihalyi puts it in *Flow: The Psychology of Optimal Experience*: 'Music ... helps organize the mind that attends to it, and therefore reduces psychic entropy, or the disorder we experience when random information interferes with goals. Listening to music wards off boredom and anxiety, and when seriously attended to, it can induce flow experiences' (Csikszentmihalyi, p. 109). Consider yourself told.

Finally, to make someone fall in love with you, you could just quiz them. Aron has created a quiz for couples to ask each other, which, when taken together as a couple, has had remarkable results. He has found that couples, even in the early phases of dating, rated themselves as much closer after sharing the answers to these questions:

1. Given the choice of anyone in the world, whom would you want as a dinner guest?
2. Would you like to be famous, in what way?
3. Before making a phone call, do you ever rehearse what you're going to say? Why?
4. What would constitute a perfect day for you?
5. When did you last sing to yourself, to someone else?
6. If you were able to live to the age of 90 and retain either the mind or body of a 30-year-old for the last 60 years of your life, which would you choose?
7. Do you have a secret hunch about how you will die?
8. Name three things you and your partner appear to have in common.
9. For what in your life do you feel most grateful?
10. If you could change anything about the way you were raised, what would it be?

In my marriage seminars, I start the day with a quiz just like this, 15 questions that couples must complete in 5 minutes. In every case, couples discover they don't know each other nearly as well as they thought they did. My results also indicate that couples who are together less than three years score far higher than couples together longer than three years.

## FIRST DATES

If you want to see how to flirt successfully, find a programme on YouTube called *First Dates*. The show has a simple premise:

a trendy restaurant is filled with singletons on their first date. The room is fitted with cameras and microphones, even in the toilets. Here you can see the secrets to successful flirting in action. They are as follows:

- Don't talk too much about yourself.
- Always be interested in your date more than anything else.
- Do not take out or use your smartphone.
- Don't discuss your ex, politics or religion.
- Mirror their body language, if they sip from a glass, you do likewise.
- Men should *always* pay for dinner on the first date.
- Finally, relax, have fun and don't take it too seriously.

In my work as a couples' therapist, I give this same advice to couples even in long-term relationships. We get so bogged down in domesticity we forget to have fun. We forget that romance is one of the nicest states we can create for each other. In the forenamed programme, I recently watched a handsome 82-year-old ex-soldier, dressed to the nines, flirt outrageously with a 73-year-old blonde. It was fantastic to watch. You are *never* too old to flirt. 'Date night' is an essential feature of a happy marriage – even if it just means turning off the TV and chatting to each other intimately.

Tracey Cox has written some excellent books on flirting, but, to be honest, the best advice I can give is that flirting is a natural instinct, so you don't have to practise it, as such, just find someone you fancy and see what comes naturally. As long as you're not being bothersome, everyone likes to be flirted with, just wait and see if they like you in return. You will know this by the way they smile. A genuine smile uses the zygomaticus major muscle group, found at the corner of the mouth – it stretches to the cheekbone, and the orbicularis oculi facial muscles, which are located around the eyes. A fake smile never moves the muscles around the eye, so this is where you need to direct your gaze when your love interest is smiling at you.

## Five Go Flirting

Psychologists Sarah E. Hill and David M. Buss from the University of Texas report that women find men more desirable when shown surrounded by women rather than when alone or with other men. Men, in contrast, rate women as being less desirable when shown with men than when shown alone or with other women.

I used this knowledge myself when I organised flirting lessons for singletons in Dublin, which I called 'Five Go Flirting'. Two men and three women went looking for love with me as their coach. The very fact that the men were already in women's company made them much more desirable to other women than if they had been by themselves. With men, status is everything so, when it comes to dating, the higher your status, the more desirable you become.

## Is That Your Bugatti Outside or Are You Just Happy To See Me?

Do displays of wealth really work on women, even in these modern times? Yes, most definitely. There have been numerous fascinating studies that prove this; one of them involved a Bugatti Veyron. If you have never heard of Bugatti, suffice to say it is one of the most expensive cars on the planet, and the fastest road car in production. It defines what is 'cool' in a car. So the experiment went like this. Regular guy pulls up beside two attractive women walking on a street in New York. He gets out of the car and asks them if they would like to hang out and show him around New York. Naturally, he is new to the area and that's his pretext for pulling up beside them. In many cases, one of the women says, 'Yeah sure, that sounds like fun.' Then he goes one further. He asks one of them, 'Tell you what, how about you just get in, and come back to my hotel, it's around the corner from here, and we can have sex.' At this point you're thinking, 'No way, she wouldn't.' Oh yes she would! Numerous girls got into the car with a total stranger, with the intention of going to his hotel and having sex. Gents, start saving.

## THE HALO EFFECT

Psychologist Edward Thorndike first used the term 'halo effect' in a 1920 paper titled 'A Constant Error in Psychological Ratings'. In the experiment described in the paper, Thorndike asked senior military officers to evaluate a number of qualities in their subordinate soldiers. These qualities included such traits as leadership skills, physical strength, intelligence, loyalty and dependability.

What he found was that high-ranking officers rated their subordinates as more intelligent, more capable and more worthy of promotion depending on how physically well built and handsome they appeared. The impact of this effect can be seen in many areas. A student who is quiet and well balanced might be perceived as brighter than the student who is loud and boisterous. This may affect how much tutoring each student receives. In court rooms around the world, it has been found that beautiful or handsome defendants are seen to be much more credible as witnesses than defendants who happen to be 'symmetrically challenged'.

In general, we tend to rate attractive people as more charming, funnier and more confident than the average person. The fact is, however, that looks have no impact on any of these characteristics. When it comes to dating, both men and women can often choose looks over substance. In my experience, this can prevent you from finding true love, so be careful how you rate your quarry.

My final piece of trickery is to have your date recall a happy memory from their childhood and tell it to you in as much detail as they can remember. In doing so, their brains will be flooded with happy chemicals. All you have to do now is to touch off them in a safe area, like near the elbow, and they will link the positive emotions from their childhood with being touched by you. Then, when you're leaving, touch them in the very same area you did previously and whisper how great it was to meet them. When they're alone and recall their date with you, they will unconsciously remember how happy they felt, and attribute this feeling to you.

## 2

# IT'S NOT ALL ABOUT SEX!

Optimism

Trust

Ex on the Beach

## LONELINESS

**M**ost of us don't like being single, to the point that the dating industry is now worth billions of dollars. We have thousands of websites dedicated to finding us love. Dating agencies promise lifelong happiness, once you trust them with your chequebook.

What lies at the root of this industry? Why do we sign up for these services in the first place?

Loneliness is the quality of being alone or, as Amy Brann, author of *Neuroscience for Coaches*, among other books, states, 'a universal human emotion or a complex set of feelings encompassing reactions to unfulfilled social needs' (Brann, p. 185). We can be surrounded by thousands of people at a concert and still feel alone. We can be at a party with our best friends and still feel alone. It's normal to feel alone at times, to feel disconnected from others and isolated. These fleeting feelings are not unhealthy. Chronic loneliness is different.

When we experience chronic loneliness, life is a struggle. We may underperform at work or university, we may withdraw from friends and we may hide our true feelings from those closest to us. Research has shown that people with chronic loneliness have elevated salivary cortisol levels. This implies that there is an increase in activation of the HPA axis.

The HPA or hypothalamic–pituitary–adrenal axis is part of our endocrine system. It regulates our digestion, immune system, mood and emotions. It's a network of connections between the hippocampus, the pituitary gland and the adrenal glands. Too much activity in the HPA axis can lead to insomnia, alcoholism, burnout and IBS (Irritable Bowel Syndrome). So is it any wonder that we're all trying to avoid loneliness?

When the HPA axis interacts with the adrenal glands, the chemical cortisol is produced. We're going to hear quite a bit about cortisol in this book so we'd better give it some attention early on. Let's do that now.

Cortisol is commonly called 'the stress hormone' because it's released when we are stressed. Cortisol plays a number of important roles in our body, though they're not all related to stress. For example, it's involved with our glucose metabolism, our blood pressure and with our immune functions. However, it has become popularised as the 'stress hormone' because it's released mainly when we are stressed.

High cortisol levels affect our ability to remember things properly as it physically shrinks the hippocampus. It also affects our sleep, which in turn makes us more stressed the next day. Not surprisingly, when couples are having problems, it becomes very challenging for them to remember what it is that they love about each other, as their memories are affected by their stress levels.

## OPTIMISM

Cortisol can affect our ability to be optimistic. When I hear a client say things like 'There's just no point' or 'Why should I bother, he will never change', I know I'm dealing with a deficiency of optimism. Yet believing that your relationship is special and has a future is essential, if you want it to thrive.

Optimism comes in two forms, realistic and unrealistic. When Sharon, a 35-year-old high-flying American executive, told me she wanted her stay-at-home husband to get a job, and become the breadwinner, I thought she was an optimist: this was good. When she told me she wanted him to get a salary of sixty thousand euro, I changed my mind. Douglas, her husband, sometimes earned only nineteen thousand euro per annum and had no intention of ever working in the kind of job that paid a larger salary. This is unrealistic optimism, and in this couple's case, had been harming their relationship for five years before they came to see me. Sharon found it difficult to accept that her salary, which was several times Doug's, was always going to be the larger salary. It didn't fit her perception of how things were supposed to be, yet that's how they were. Sadly, despite my best efforts, this couple went their separate ways.

Optimism tends to show up on brain scans as activity in the left hemisphere of the brain. When we are in a positive state of mind there is activity in the left frontal gyrus while the right inferior frontal gyrus responds to bad news. Pessimism is rooted in the right-hand side of our brain. Just in case you ever wondered!

Suzanne Segerstrom, the American psychologist, did some experiments in 2007 to research optimism using what's known as the stroop test. The stroop test was popularised in the last few years by a leading games manufacturer. You're shown a screen that has the word 'red' on it, but the word is written in green. Your job is to say the colour of the writing and not the word itself. Segerstrom surveyed 48 college students about their levels of optimism before administering the test. She found that there was a corollary between how much people rated themselves as optimists and the amount of time they persisted at the task. Optimists stayed longer on the test than those who rated themselves as pessimists. Is this why optimists are more successful than pessimists, they just don't quit when things get tough?

I've worked with many single people who were trying to find love. One of the challenges I set them was to bring them to a busy bar and watch how they interacted with the opposite sex. The one characteristic that distinguished successful clients from unsuccessful clients was the quality of optimism. When my clients believed that they would meet Mr or Ms Right, they usually did. They were so full of confidence that it acted like a magnet literally dragging people towards them. Their smiles would light up the room and everyone would take notice. The people I couldn't help tended to stare at the floor. No one ever came over to chat to these clients, funnily enough.

Mike was a 40-year-old single guy; shy but very friendly if you can accept the inherent contradiction. He was a farmer, so he didn't have that many opportunities to meet women. He was a handsome man, wispy blond hair, boyish looks, and he had looked after himself through strength training. His biggest problem was the belief he had that *every* woman who looked at him fancied him. No matter how many sessions we worked together, he persisted in his belief that each and every woman that glanced in his direction did so because he was irresistible. The last time we spoke, Mike was still single. There's optimism, and then there is Mike's version of optimism.

To become more optimistic you can do a number of things:

- Choose to think positively about any situation that is bothering you or causing you stress.
- Brainstorm ways in which this problem is good for you, building your character or helping you grow.
- Use your imagination to visualise positive outcomes to the situation you face.
- Use long-term potentiation to your advantage.

Long-term potentiation is the name given to how cells grow stronger, and make more connections in response to you choosing to think the same thoughts. For example, if you want to increase trust between you and your partner, make a decision to repeat, about 30 times per day, the words 'I trust my partner because ...', then list out reasons to trust them. This will literally change the internal structure of your brain. Remember, what you give attention to, grows.

Or as the Dalai Lama put it: 'Through mental training you can increase positive thoughts and can reduce negative thoughts. I can tell you, with conviction; through effort we can change our mental attitudes.'

## GRATITUDE

Numerous studies have concluded that gratitude is very good for us. Adopting an attitude of gratitude has been found to reduce stress and can prevent the activation of the HPA axis. We tend to be physically healthier, and relate to our lovers with more warmth, than if we focus on what we don't have. When researchers asked a group of people to keep gratitude journals for one month, they noted a significant increase in their levels of optimism compared to how they felt before the study began.

## TRUST

Whenever we act in a way that our partners think is untrustworthy, we place what educator Stephen Covey describes as a 'tax' on the relationship. If you come home late from work five nights in a row, with no explanation, this will place a stress on your relationship. Tensions will build and anxiety levels will increase. This will trigger the release of cortisol. Your wife may not be able to sleep properly. She may start to lose motivation in work. The absence of trust in a relationship is highly significant. Trust matters.

What is trust? Trust can be defined as a 'strong belief in the reliability of someone or something' (Brann, p. 36). When we spend time with someone in the dating phase of our relationship, we are all the time deciding if this person is someone we want to give our body, resources or future to. These are big questions. After marriage, when the commitment has been given, we sometimes think we no longer need to earn our lover's trust. This is a myth. In fact the opposite is true: at all times, especially after a marriage, you should be working towards keeping your partner's trust.

## THE LAW OF RECIPROCITY

Trust reduces activation in the amygdala, which is where much of our emotional life is regulated. The amygdala also processes fear more quickly than anything else, so a reduction in activity in this area leaves us feeling safer and more content. Trust increases activation in the reward centres of the brain such as the mesolimbic reward centre. Usually when our lover does something that increases our trust in them, we feel an urge to reciprocate. This is known as the law of reciprocity. This law states that when someone does something nice or kind for us, we feel a natural inclination to reciprocate. This law is a fundamental law of human nature. Once we reciprocate, trust starts to grow between us. But when trust is broken and we feel anxious or afraid as a result, our ability to plan a future together diminishes. We hesitate in making big decisions like buying a house or planning a baby.

To restore trust we can surround ourselves with people who care about us, as our levels of fear and anxiety actually diminish, thanks to the influence of oxytocin. If we come to a long-term relationship with significant trust issues, our brains can be helped to relax if we allow ourselves to receive lots of physical affection from our partners and even our friends.

Interestingly, when we think our partners are going to meet our needs, even sometime in the future, we receive a hit of dopamine. This feels good. But then once we find out that this need, whatever it was, will not be met by them (maybe they are too tired to give you that massage), our pain receptors light up instead, and we start to focus on what's negative in the relationship. This doesn't feel so good.

When we trust someone unconditionally, the septal area of the brain is involved. But where we trust someone with 'strings attached', then the ventral tegmental area is activated instead. Trust has two forms, it seems.

The chemical oxytocin has been studied in relation to trust. Oxytocin floods the brain when two people are making love or when a woman is giving birth, two high-trust experiences. The charismatic neuroeconomist Paul J. Zak has carried out a number of studies into oxytocin and concluded that there are certain things we can do to increase trust. One of them involves giving away some of our money.

Zak did the following social experiment. Subjects were given an amount of money, say $10, and asked if they wanted to give away all, some or none of this sum to another player that they couldn't see. Why would they do such a thing? Because they were told that the other player had the chance to do the same thing and depending on what *both* players did, this would affect how they would be rewarded. If both players opted to give away all of their money, then they would be rewarded, but if one player kept his money and gave nothing away, then no reward would be received. Throughout the world, the results are almost always the same. People who give away their money show an increase in trust with the other player, despite being a total stranger.

Oxytocin makes us feel more empathy towards others. It increases the levels of warmth that we experience with people. If you want to see how oxytocin feels right now, give your partner a hug for over 30 seconds, and wait. That nice warm feeling you both have? That's oxytocin. If you don't have a partner, ask someone you like in the coffee shop to give you a hug. What's the worst that can happen?

I once wore a T-shirt to a dance festival as a social experiment with the slogan 'Free Hugs' printed clearly on the front, in big, bold, white letters. I was inundated with hugs from both women *and* men. I was a very happy person. Oxytocin is one of the best drugs there is, and it's completely free.

## Ex on the Beach

If you believe you're being lied to, your anterior cingulate cortex will detect this, and activate your amygdala. This is what causes that uneasy feeling you get in your stomach, when something your lover has said doesn't quite fit. The activation of the amygdala serves as a warning bell that we need to pay heed to as quickly as possible. We can't function properly unless we do so.

There's a reality show on MTV called *Ex on the Beach*. I must confess it's my guilty pleasure. The premise of the show is simple. Eight attractive singletons, mostly models, are taken to a stunning villa near the sandy beaches of sunny Cancun. There they live in blissful harmony, flirting and frolicking with one another. When they least expect it, three of the group are asked to go to the beach and wait. Eventually, like a sea god or goddess, one of their exes emerges from the sea, in slow motion, of course, with the sun glistening off their tanned and sculpted bodies, and then moves into the villa with them. At this point, everyone has kissed someone else, so the arrival of the ex really disrupts the group dynamics, and not in a good way.

This continues until all eight housemates have their exes living with them. The tension is unbearable to watch. The lies the boys had told the girls come back to haunt them, as once their exes arrive, they usually lose interest in the current girlfriend in favour of the ex they had a history with.

Stress levels always peak when the ex first arrives, as jealousy and fear set into the new girlfriend or boyfriend. Watching amygdala activation and HPA axes being set alight is awful, but fascinating. Faces redden, pulses race and hearts jump when each model sees their ex flirt with the other housemates. Jealousy and insecurity are two sides of the same coin.

Talk about exploitation! As I said, it's my guilty pleasure.

In relationships, we see trust-building in the form of gift-giving and lovemaking. The more a man shows a woman that he is trustworthy, by being faithful *and* by giving her access to his financial resources, the more likely she is to return her trust in him through sex or affection. This sounds weird but has been proved throughout the ages. All that has changed is the type of gifts men give to women. In days of old, gifts consisted of mules and donkeys. Thankfully, if nothing else, at least we're a bit classier now.

To maintain trust we need to be consistent in what we say or do. If we promise to help our partner get the money they need to fund a new college course but then renege on that when the time comes, trust will take a nosedive. If we say we will be happy to have children in our marriage but once a baby comes along we act like a spoilt child ourselves, trust will disappear.

Trust is a finite resource. In my experience, once we break trust it's very hard to get it back fully. What I suggest to my clients is that both speak openly about the value placed on certain activities such as timekeeping or following through on commitments. Only through open and honest dialogue can we expect trust to be fostered sufficiently, to help us sustain a happy marriage throughout our lifetimes.

## What's a Mirror Neuron?

It was a hot sticky night in Vancouver. The huge crowd was singing as one voice, all sixty thousand of them. U2 were belting out their classic ballad 'I Still Haven't Found What I'm Looking For'. The Edge was walking nonchalantly down the runway in the centre of the stage, strumming his guitar gracefully, as he does, smiling at his adoring fans. Then the crowd watched in shock as the Edge fell off the stage. Everyone gasped. They winced and grimaced, feeling both his pain and his embarrassment. (It seemed he hadn't found the stage.) Their reaction was caused by the activation of mirror neurons.

Now, while I'm not a fan of experimenting on animals, one of the most important findings in brain science involved monkeys. In a lab in Parma, Italy, a group of neuroscientists, Giacomo Rizzolatti, Leonardo Fogassi and Vittorio Gallese, placed recording electrodes into the inferior frontal cortex of the macaque monkey. The monkeys were linked up to a machine that made a noise when they reached for a peanut. One day a graduate student who was eating his lunch heard the machine beep. However, the monkey hadn't moved. The scientists were baffled. They only expected the machine to make a noise when the monkeys reached for or ate the peanut. What was happening was the monkeys' neurons were firing just by watching the student eat his own lunch. This was the discovery of 'mirror neurons', 'a type of neuron that fires when an action is observed in another neuron' (Brann, p. 93). Later research proved that humans have more sophisticated versions of this amazing system.

The discovery of mirror neurons has profound implications for our relationships. They allow us to 'intuit' what another is feeling. They allow us to create rapport with those around us and they give us the feeling of belonging to groups. In intimate relationships, when our lover is in pain, we too can share this pain. When they bang their elbow on their funny bone, we sense some of their discomfort. Mirror neurons facilitate this process.

In one study involving people being shown boxing matches while inside MRI machines, half of the subjects were told to imagine what the boxer was feeling, the other half were told just to watch the boxing match passively. When the brain scans were analysed afterwards, it was found that those who had imagined the boxers' feelings had activation in multiple brain areas, and the connections between them got bigger as time went on. Essentially, they had 'felt' some of the boxers' pain.

Some neuroscientists are conjecturing that mirror neurons are also important for:

- Understanding the minds of others
- Feeling more empathy for people
- Helping us to understand the motivation behind other people's behaviour

Developing more empathy for your partner is a sure-fire way of improving your relationship. By tuning into what he or she is feeling, you have a great opportunity to maintain the love between you both. However, from a negative perspective, mirror neurons may fire off when our partner is angry, disgusted or feeling rejected. This means that your positive mood might not last too long if your partner is feeling angry and they happen to be in your company. At this point it can be hard to separate out what you're feeling from what they're feeling and to give yourself the space you need to regain homeostasis (the status quo).

Without mirror neurons, parents wouldn't understand the complex nature of their baby's cries and know how to comfort the baby. Mirror neurons allow us to respond appropriately in groups so that when one person looks up from their handout at the presenter, we all tend to. The Mexican wave that takes place in football stadiums around the world couldn't happen without them. When we play sports as a team, and someone makes a huge faux pas, like an own goal, we share their regret and embarrassment as if it was us that made the mistake. Cooperation between tribes and families takes place due to mirror-neuron activation. When I, as a therapist, cross my arms or unfold my legs in sync with my client, it's the work of mirror neurons. I am perceived as more empathic as a result.

As a therapist, being able to interpret a client's body language is crucial to offering them what psychologist Carl Rogers called 'unconditional positive regard'. In numerous studies, this one feature of the therapeutic relationship has been found to be more important in determining the success of the therapeutic intervention than anything else. No matter how qualified or experienced the therapist is, if they are unable to accurately assess the client's feelings, then therapy will not work with that client. It's only because of the existence of mirror neurons that this is possible.

The easiest way for *you* to activate someone's mirror neurons is by yawning. Try it for yourself. I bet even the fact that I have primed you, by saying the word 'yawn', has caused your mind to think it wants to yawn. Am I right?

## EMPATHY

According to psychotherapist Louis Cozolino, 'The everyday understanding of empathy consists of a muddle of resonance, attunement and sympathy. In order to have empathy, we need to maintain an awareness of our inner world as we imagine the inner world of others' (Cozolino, p. 203). In order to understand what you are feeling, I need to call to mind, at an unconscious level, any similar experiences I have had that may help me know your mind.

When couples come to me for therapy, one of the traits I'm scanning for is empathy. Frequently a client will be in tears discussing the heartbreak caused by her husband's affair. Does he reach out and try to soothe her, does he look ashamed or is he defensive? These reactions can predict whether the couple have a future together or not. By sensing and acting on our instinct to comfort our partners when they need us, we deactivate their stress systems, and give them a feeling of security and safety. Doing this frequently is a key to strengthening the bond between you both.

One technique I use in my own practice to create empathy between couples is to have one member of the couple leave the room and wait downstairs. Then I ask the person remaining, a husband, Nick, for example, to sit in his wife's empty chair. I then resume the remainder of the session with the following introduction: 'So now that you are in Nancy's chair, I'm going to presume you are Nancy. So I would like you to answer the remainder of these questions as if you were her.'

- Nancy, how did you feel before coming today?
- What do you think of what Nick has been saying so far?
- Do you agree with his viewpoint?
- What do you think are the challenges in your relationship?
- What are the strengths?
- What do you want to change in the relationship in the future?

Then I swap around the exercise when the wife returns and I send the husband downstairs. This is a remarkably effective way to find out what your partner is thinking and feeling and, while it has its limitations, I am amazed how easily people can think like their partner.

## THE IMPORTANCE OF NOVELTY

In the early phases of most relationships, each member of the couple is trying to impress the other. In the process, men may make a big effort to take their lover on interesting and exciting dates. Eventually, however, they settle into a familiar pattern of doing the same activities over and over again. It might be going for walks, going to the cinema or, if you have children, streaming a movie from your smartphone on to your smart TV.

However, this isn't wise if you want your relationship to last. Brain scientists have discovered that the same parts of our brain that respond to pleasure also respond to surprise.

Dr Gregory Berns of Emory University used fMRI scanners to study neural responses to different stimuli. He focused in on the nucleus accumbens or the pleasure centre of the brain. He discovered that unpredictability caused the pleasure centre to 'light up' with neural activity.

In the experiment, researchers squirted either water or juice into volunteers' mouths while the volunteers' brain activity was monitored. When squirts of fluid were delivered at unpredictable intervals, the pleasure centre activated more strongly than when squirts were predictable, regardless of whether the fluid was juice or water.

In other words, if you want to stay happily married, make sure you surprise each other frequently. Boredom with married life is cited by some people as their main reason for divorce. More and more, research reveals that people in perfectly healthy marriages are lacking novelty to such an extent that they are prepared to change the person they are married to, just to feel happy again.

To prevent your partner wanting to swap you for someone else, perhaps you could try abseiling, archery, boating, ballooning, dancing, fencing: need I go on? When in doubt, remember what Robin Williams taught us in *Dead Poets Society*: 'Carpe Diem'.

To sum up: if you want to get laid – develop an attitude of confidence, optimism and adventure. When you meet people you like, watch for pupil dilation, then get them to hug you as much as possible. The oxytocin that floods their brain will make them trust you even more and hopefully that, combined with your stunning good looks, will make them believe, thanks to the halo effect (Chapter 1) that you are great in bed. When finally you do get them into bed, keep it novel and interesting. Don't let boredom creep in, whatever you do.

# 3

# A Quick Guide to the Brain: Part One

The Amygdala or Gorilla

The Anterior Cingulate Cortex or Inner Sherlock

Good v Evil

## INSIDE YOUR BRAIN

**W**elcome to the brain. Your brain has many different and complex parts, with names some people find a bit esoteric. I think the best way I can teach you is to refer to them by words or names you may already recognise.

In this brief section, we're going to look at how to manage these different areas of the brain should they start to get you into trouble.

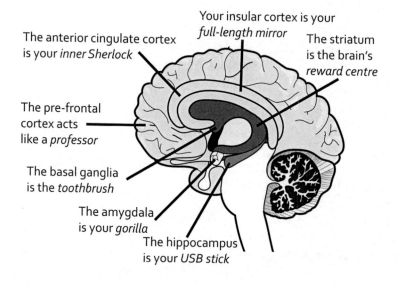

Your insular cortex is your *full-length mirror*

The anterior cingulate cortex is your *inner Sherlock*

The striatum is the brain's *reward centre*

The pre-frontal cortex acts like a *professor*

The basal ganglia is the *toothbrush*

The amygdala is your *gorilla*

The hippocampus is your *USB stick*

## THE AMYGDALA OR GORILLA

This is a small almond-shaped brain part that manages our emotions. It gives preference to fear over anything else. So if you're feeling three or four emotions at the same time, this brain part will process fear faster than the others. It's a primitive part of the brain. When you see a speeding car coming your way, the amygdala activates and tells you to get of there, fast. It doesn't stop to think or analyse. It wants you to act immediately.

The amygdala is super-fast and super-primal. From now on, we will call it your 'gorilla'.

Gorillas take no nonsense from anyone. Gorillas take a long time to calm down if they are angry. They mark their territory clearly and they tend to be hungry, often.

Gorillas tend to react first, and ask questions later. They get spooked easily. They can be quite defensive and over-sensitive at times.

Keeping our gorilla under control is a key task in maintaining a healthy relationship. It's difficult to rein in the effects of gorilla activation once it begins; the best thing you can do is to prevent it activating in the first place.

To do this you need to establish good routines for your life; chaos is your enemy. Agree when you will discuss your relationship and do this on a regular basis. Check in at least once every two weeks to see if there are any issues bubbling under the surface that you may be picking up on. If there have been issues there, your gorilla will activate but you won't understand why.

Sleep well – sleep keeps the gorilla under control by maintaining a healthy amount of hormones in the body.

Establish healthy routines so that you exercise well and rest frequently. Avoid unnecessary stress, as it makes controlling your gorilla that much harder.

Eat properly and avoid sugary or processed foods. A bad diet will reduce your ability to process information accurately, leading to an over-sensitive gorilla.

Finally, develop an attitude of optimism. It releases endorphins your brain needs to make you feel better. Optimism helps your gorilla to relax.

## The Pre-frontal Cortex or Professor

The part of our brain that controls most of what we do each day is called the pre-frontal cortex. If this is malfunctioning, it can lead to all sorts of problems. From now on we will call it your 'professor'.

Professors are supposed to be analytical, critical and rational. We tend to trust them. The professor is located in the frontal lobes of the brain. The frontal lobes are involved in inhibiting inappropriate behaviour, in decision-making, and in planning. For this reason, damage to the professor commonly leads to an inability to behave in ways that are socially acceptable. If the damage occurs in childhood, individuals may never develop any understanding of moral behaviour. When an injury happens in adulthood, the person may realise what is socially required but may still be unable to behave in an acceptable way.

The function of this part of the brain is to carry out complex tasks. Judgements and decisions could be impaired following its injury as these are the parts of the brain that enable a person to think about future outcomes, in the light of what happened in the past, allowing the probable best course of action to be chosen.

A healthy professor helps us make important decisions. Should I stay in this relationship? Will my life be better if I get a new job? Should I allow my family to treat me the way they do? All these questions require deliberate thought and action. The professor's job is to weigh up the benefits of any decision against the possible consequences.

Damage to the professor is relatively common, since this area is right behind the forehead. If you or your partner played contact sports, you may have damaged this area of your brain. Even falling from a bicycle with no helmet may cause damage to this area. Never let a child ride a bike unless they are wearing a helmet. My own brother fell from his bike when he was eight years old. He wasn't wearing a helmet. His personality changed fundamentally after the accident.

## MANAGING THE PROFESSOR

When we are anxious, we tend to activate the 'periaqueductal gray' or PAG, which is a brain region responsible for acute anxiety management. So to restore balance we need to take a different time perspective on the problems in question. Maybe they don't need to be resolved right away. Perhaps you can both discuss them again another time. Asking questions of each other such as 'Is this situation a threat right now or can it wait?' or 'If we do nothing about this now, will we still be okay?' are important for gaining clarity and allowing your professor to do its job.

## THE HYPOTHALAMUS OR THERMOSTAT

Essentially, this brain area controls our bodily functions. It manages the endocrine system and the nervous system. The hypothalamus releases many chemicals into our body and brain to make sure we are functioning properly. It regulates hunger, thirst, sleep and stress. There is also a link to our emotions in this brain area but as of yet the research does not point to it having a huge impact on our conscious behaviours. I am going to refer to it as your 'thermostat'.

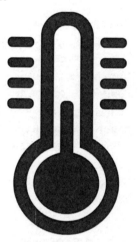

## THE ANTERIOR CINGULATE CORTEX OR INNER SHERLOCK

When you think of Sherlock Holmes you think of a detective, someone who can uncover clues about what's happening in a dangerous situation. The anterior cingulate cortex or ACC is one of the most active parts of the brain when we argue. Some people even think that this is the link between the unconscious and the conscious brain. It may send messages from the unconscious to the conscious at lightning-fast speeds. The inner Sherlock scans our environment, both internal and external, to see what threats or conflicts exist. If it spots something, it tells the rest of the brain to sit up and take notice.

If the in-laws are coming to visit in a few days and you don't enjoy their company, you might become anxious at an unconscious level. The inner Sherlock will send messages to your gorilla and put it on alert. However, you might not know this has happened. You will just feel on edge. You may overreact to your husband's daily behaviours but not know why.

To manage the inner Sherlock you need to pause, take time out and examine the evidence for what you are thinking or feeling. Writing down your beliefs or assumptions can help you to understand if what you're thinking is accurate or not. Aim for accuracy as much as you can.

## The Hippocampus or USB Stick

Context is everything when it comes to resolving arguments. How tired, hungry or stressed you are can make all the difference to your ability to resolve them. Whatever has gone before the argument shapes our ability to process it properly. A simple argument over housework can be exacerbated if there has been a sequence of criticism before it.

The brain area that helps us put things in context is the 'USB stick'. This area acts as a storage centre for all our previous memories. To make sure this area of the brain is working for us, and not against us, we can employ the following techniques:

- Review what has come before the argument: this is where we ask ourselves if there is another reason we are upset besides the topic being argued about. You might come home from a long, stressful holiday with your children, walk into your kitchen, notice a piece of crockery left unwashed from before the trip and immediately criticise your partner for not being tidy enough. The trigger was crockery but the real problem was the stress from the holiday.

• Define the emotional stakes – without realising it we can carry around expectations about how an argument might proceed based on previous experiences. For example, in the past your husband had a habit of walking away from you, leaving you feeling abandoned and confused. Today you're arguing about money, and you sense he is about to walk away once more so you become tense and angry. The 'USB stick' has just activated and flooded your brain with memories from the past. Now you overreact and start to accuse him of walking away, even though he hasn't budged from where he's standing.

It can be hard to do this in practice, but we need to check in with ourselves regularly to see if what we are feeling is accurate or is an older memory coming back to haunt us.

## THE STRIATUM OR REWARD CENTRE

The striatum is where the brain measures and releases rewards. I'm going to refer to it as your 'reward centre', illustrated by the cupcake below. Remember, the brain is a pleasure-seeking mechanism. It's *always* hungry for rewards. It works the same way in a relationship. The brain is constantly asking itself, 'What am I getting out of

this?' Relationships tend to fall apart when someone decides that the rewards are not enough to justify the work involved in maintaining homeostasis.

When we argue, we move further and further from the likelihood of getting a reward, so tension builds up internally. This stress is experienced all over the body and not just in the brain. Blood pressures rise, hearts pump faster and generally we feel much more anxious during the argument, possibly resulting in an outburst of anger or rage.

To move past an argument, we need to know that when we do, there will be some incentive waiting for us. This might be a simple gesture such as a hug, a cuddle or a lingering kiss. Couples that are enduring ongoing problems without any resolution find it very difficult to see any results for their efforts. To break out of this cycle there are a few strategies we can employ:

- Take a long-term time perspective: in other words, plan for happier times in the future and imagine what they may be like. You might promise yourselves that after this argument has been fully resolved you will plan a weekend away together, a nice meal, or just sharing a bath. Remind yourselves that you have more to offer each other than unpleasant comments during rows.

- Accept the olive branch – when one person is trying to offer an apology, even if it's only a gesture like suggesting they make you a coffee, learn to accept these gestures and see them for what they are. It can be hard to see a positive side to your partner when you are angry with them, but let's face it, they must have one, or you wouldn't be with them in the first place.
- Be clear on the reasons why – when you are both in a good space, discuss the reasons you are together. What is it you both like about each other? What do you get from your spouse that you might not get from anyone else? Write these down some-place safe and recall them when you're finding it hard to see a way forward from the argument. By recalling the purpose of your relationship you can get back on course more easily and gain a different perspective.

Using all three of these strategies regularly will give you both that all-important dopamine boost that your brain craves. Remember dopamine is the sugar in our doughnut. Everything feels better when we get regular hits of dopamine.

## THE INSULAR CORTEX OR FULL-LENGTH MIRROR

To get a sense of how we appear in our new clothes, we look into a mirror. The insular cortex is similar to a full-length mirror; it helps us understand who we are. It's where most brain scientists think that consciousness can be located. It gives us a sense of ourselves.

When we argue, we may have a gut feeling that something isn't right. This feeling has its origins in the full-length mirror. Tuning into this sensation is really important for us. It might not always be correct, but if we ignore what it's telling us, we may feel that we have done ourselves a disservice. Trust your gut instinct as much as you can.

## THE BASAL GANGLIA OR TOOTHBRUSH

When you brush your teeth or comb your hair, you don't stop to think about it, it comes naturally. You could say it's a habit. Habits are managed by cells called the basal ganglia. We have billions of them in our brains. They help you drive your car, cycle your bike, and type emails. When we are addicted to sugar, cigarettes or alcohol, it's the basal ganglia that control these addictions (in conjunction with other brain regions). To remind you that the basal ganglia are all about habits, I'm going to call them your 'toothbrush'.

## GOOD V EVIL

Two chemicals that you will hear more about throughout this book are dopamine and cortisol.

**Dopamine** makes us feel happy. It literally is that simple to understand.

**Cortisol** make us feel stressed. It can also keep us alert but usually we don't like how it makes us feel.
To help us understand how the brain works:

- The amygdala is now your gorilla
- The pre-frontal cortex is now your professor
- The anterior cingulate cortex is now your inner Sherlock

- The hippocampus has become your USB stick
- Your striatum is your reward centre
- Your insular cortex is your full-length mirror
- The basal ganglia are your toothbrush

# 4

# THE BRAIN IN LOVE (AND LUST)

Making Marriage Last

What Is True Love?

Attraction

## What Happens when We Fall in Love?

So long as we are given up to the throng of desires with their constant hopes and fears ... we never obtain lasting happiness or peace. – Schopenhauer

The prairie vole is a pretty unique rodent. When it mates, it mates for life. It chooses one other vole to give all its attention to, to nest with, to take care of, and to have sex with. Scientists have been studying the prairie vole for years in an attempt to discover the secret to lifelong monogamy. If only our love lives were as simple as that of the prairie vole.

When we fall in love we are all-consumed by our lover, time slows down and we may enter an altered state of reality. Our brains are awash with chemicals that distort our perception of our partner's bad habits. Nothing they do seems like a problem and we believe our undying love can conquer all.

Most therapists only work with couples in distress, when the two thundering stallions of romance and lust have long since left the stable. I, on the other hand, have the task of helping couples (who are literally mad with love) to gain some perspective on the strengths and weaknesses of their relationships *before* they marry.

In one such private marriage course, I realised that the slender, stunning brunette in my office looked familiar to me. In fact, she was an English celebrity I was a huge fan of. In that session, as in most other private sessions, I explored the couple's views and expectations about marriage and child-rearing. As the couple were together less than three years, I knew that getting them to see any negatives about their relationship would be a challenge. Why so? To answer this, we need to learn about anthropologist Helen Fisher and her startling findings about love and lust.

Using MRI and fMRI machines, Fisher conducted experiments to see which parts of her subjects' brains would 'light up' when she showed them photographs of their lovers. What she found was that different brain parts activated, depending on how long the couples were together. In other words there *is* a difference in the brain between lust and love.

So what did she learn? She discovered that when any two individuals fall in love, rather than destiny bringing them together and guaranteeing their future happiness, it was more a case of their brains being flooded with a number of powerful chemicals. These chemicals include norepinephrine and dopamine. High levels of dopamine give us focused attention and better motivation. Dopamine also suppresses appetite, provides us with feelings of ecstasy and creates neural pathways that allow us to focus all our attention on our partners.

Norepinephrine produces sleeplessness and excessive energy. This same chemical increases your ability to remember the smaller details of your lover's life and hold on to those memories.

You might also be familiar with the brain chemical serotonin. Serotonin is linked to obsessive thinking and what Fisher found was that many of her subjects who were in love had the same brain activity as people suffering from OCD! So in other words, being in love with someone makes you obsessed with them.

When I was in college, many years ago, a young couple in my class fell in love. This wasn't that unusual. What was unusual and perhaps a little worrying was how the couple expressed this love. I never forget the day when Shane and Lisa arrived into a theology lecture on sexual morality, decked out in bright-blue T-shirts and matching bright-blue baseball caps, with the words 'I love you Shane' and 'I love you Lisa' printed clearly in bold red writing on both T-shirts and caps. Oblivious to the looks of confusion and disgust from the Catholic priest and their fellow classmates, this young 19-year-old couple spent their first year of college in sheer bliss, holding hands and gazing lovingly into each other's eyes at every opportunity.

Romantic love is characterised by four factors: intrusive thinking, obsession, intense energy and a lack of appetite. What we usually see portrayed in Hollywood movies is the obsessive version of love. If this image of love is all we know, and all we base our judgements on, and we have no other frame of reference to guide us, is it any wonder that so many millions of us are still single, or living our lives in unhappy marriages?

The truth is that being in love causes people to make poor decisions. The professor, which controls logical thinking, is unable to withstand the effects of the love chemicals. People elope from their families and give up their careers just to be with that special person: such is the power of romantic love.

Does this mean that our brains are able to intuitively 'know' when we have met our 'Mr' or 'Ms Right'? Well, not quite. If that was the case, then no one would get divorced. Given that some estimates put divorce rates at 30–50 per cent in the Western hemisphere, clearly our brains are not to be trusted.

If our brains can't be trusted, why did evolution give us such powerful tools in the first place? Why do we fall in love at all?

On 26 January 2014, in a tiny waiting room in a Dublin maternity hospital, a doting father was nervously holding his newborn baby. The baby was just five minutes old and looked a bit alien-like (yet beautiful as all babies do). Despite the rollercoaster of emotions that followed, this father finally made sense of every philosophical question he had ever pondered. Questions like 'Why are we here?' and 'What's it all about?' suddenly made sense.

This fragile human being had awakened a primal instinct in him, the like of which he had never thought possible: the urge to protect, to nurture and to love. That father was this book's author and that baby was my daughter, Éabha.

Once a man becomes a parent, he often notices a huge drop in his sex drive, his lust for his partner can dissipate and his awareness of his role as protector of the family takes over. His brain chemistry changes radically. Instead of dopamine and norepinephrine surges, oxytocin and other opiates start to be produced through physical contact with his child.

Oxytocin, which is nicknamed the 'cuddle-chemical', is more present in women than in men. It's especially present when a woman is giving birth and allows the woman to bond more effectively with her baby. Breastfeeding also releases oxytocin in women, which can occasionally make the experience enjoyable for both mother and baby.

When new parents are being kind to one another, rather than feeling the desire to have sex, each might feel more like being tender and nurturing. This is oxytocin at work.

'Gaia' was the name the Greeks gave to Mother Earth. 'Terra' was how she was known to the Romans. Whatever we like to call this planet and the life force that sustains us, I can't help but be struck by the incredible design that is behind all of Life. Life wants us to find a mate, to become pregnant and repeat the eternal cycle of life begetting life. But once this has happened, nature gives us a little break.

The 'being in love' phase only lasts a short time. Fisher found that many of her interviewees stayed in love for a period of two to three years but no more than that. Once we have mated, we don't need the same electrical impulses or cocktail of chemicals flowing through our brains. Thus we shift to a more protective role. This experience can last up to three years before the urge to reproduce may hit us again. That's not to say that new parents don't have sex after a baby, of course they do, they just don't feel the urge as strongly.

While Fisher was working away in Rutgers University where she was based, and completely unbeknown to her, a team of researchers in London was also trying to identify where love might register in the human brain. Andreas Bartels and Semir Zeki found that when their subjects were shown photographs of their lovers, while undergoing MRI scans, an area of the brain called the caudate nucleus became activated. This was great news for Fisher who had the very same results thousands of miles away in her own lab.

The London researchers were working with people who were in love for an average of two and a half years, whereas Fisher's subjects were together about seven months. The London team found more activity in the inner Sherlock and the full-length mirror. Some of the couples that were in longer relationships showed activity in both brain areas. Fisher postulates that as a relationship deepens, the brain areas associated with emotions and memory respond in new ways. What this means she has yet to discover, but nonetheless it's fascinating to finally know where love 'is' in the brain. Not quite the stuff of poets and troubadours, mind you.

## MAKING MARRIAGE LAST

I'm often asked when teaching couples how to make their marriage a success, 'So if romantic love only lasts a maximum of three years, how do some couples in their dotage manage to look so "in love"?' The answer is that falling in love is caused by nature; staying in love is caused by us. I'm going to sum up briefly what all the great relationship experts, from William James to John Gottman, believe are the secrets to staying in love. I'm going to do so with two words, so brace yourselves, and sit down if you happen to be standing on a train or on a bus somewhere: the secret to lifelong happiness in a relationship is *Respect* and *Excitement*.

When you respect your partner and feel respected by them, your brain maintains a stable equilibrium of chemicals, which manages your emotions effectively and fuels optimism and posi- tive thinking. Even in the height of conflict, if you believe that your partner respects you, you are less likely to be negative, to make nasty comments or be deliberately hurtful.

When it comes to excitement, if you each try to excite one another regularly, your brains will flood with adrenaline and dopamine and both chemicals will cause you to feel more attracted to one another. In experiments involving rope bridges, it's been discovered that we rate people as more attractive the more adrenaline that's released into our bloodstreams (due to the danger associated with the activity we are doing together). This is why television dating shows try to simulate romance by using rock climbing or horse riding as perfect first-date experiences.

So if you want to stay happily married for the next 30 years, get off the couch, book in for a weekend of escapades at your nearest adventure centre, and get moving.

## ARE SWINGERS' BRAINS DIFFERENT THAN MONOGAMISTS' BRAINS?

Recently the 'glamorous' world of swinging has been thrust upon us again by newspapers, TV shows and the Internet, seeming to portray sex parties as positive experiences for couples who are open-minded enough to cope with watching their loved one engage in a bit of horizontal jogging with total strangers. So what do swingers' brains look like? Are they different than yours? Perhaps you're a swinger. Do you think your brain is different than that of a monogamist?

To date, no one seems to have thought to analyse swingers' brains. But let's see if we can make an educated guess as to what might be happening when people are involved in the 'lifestyle', as it's known. I did ask Helen Fisher to work on this with me but she declined my offer – Helen, there's still time!

At most swingers' parties, groups of couples meet, exchange pleasantries and within a very short timeframe are having sex with each other's partners. Are these people sex addicts or just normal people with high sex drives and incredibly trusting relationships?

While I have never been to such parties, I have worked with a number of clients who were sex addicts and who often took part in sex parties. One client, a woman in her mid forties, described her story in the following way.

> It started off with me being bored with my husband. We had lost interest in each other sexually. To fix this we decided to try and spice things up by involving a female friend of mine in a sex session. That went well, we all had a lot of fun, and bizarrely I felt no jealousy at all when he was with her. I wasn't sure why that was. A few weeks later my friend got in touch to say that she was going to a small 'lifestyle' party and would we like to come. I jumped at the chance.
>
> When we got there, I was overwhelmed by the attention I received from the men. I felt so desired, so wanted, so needed, even. After a few hours of drinking and flirting, I sobered up and took stock of what was happening. There I was, a middle-aged woman, on a large bed, with three men and two women having sex with me. My husband was in a different room doing the same with other people.
>
> Within a week, I was having daily fantasies about the party. Shortly afterwards, and without my husband's knowledge, I went to another party. There I was a different person. I was aggressive, I was pushy, I was demanding. I had sex with about ten men and three women that night. I was insatiable.

All sounds wonderful, doesn't it, and except for the dishonesty around not telling her husband about the second sex party, what's the problem? Let's look inside this client's brain, hypothetically.

We know that sex releases powerful chemicals in our brains. In women, oxytocin is the main chemical that creates a bond with the woman's lover. In men, it's vasopressin that binds the man to the woman. When we meet people we are attracted to, our eyes register the stimulus, which sends messages to the occipital region, which sends messages to the ventral reward centre. The electrical impulses that course through our neural connections create waves of excitement. The thermostat that controls our breathing works harder and we notice how dry our mouth becomes, how sweaty our palms feel and how flushed our face becomes. All these symptoms of lust then register in the micro expressions on our face.

If my client has dopamine and oxytocin rushes with multiple different partners, how might this affect her brain wiring? Is casual sex with multiple partners (at the same time) good for the human brain?

Human beings need to feel loved, to feel a sense of belonging and to feel important. Now imagine having an in-depth conversation with one of your best friends where you discuss intimate aspects of your lives. You feel more connected as a result. Now, just as you are concluding this chat, seven total strangers walk into the room, sit down with you both and proceed to repeat back to you everything that you had just shared together in private. Would this experience be positive or negative for you?

For many of us, sex is an act of intimacy. Yes I know that people drink too much and have casual sex with people they don't know. But most of the time this isn't premeditated, and only involves two people. As a result it's easier to forget it, suppress it or blame it on the alcohol. In my experience, many people who have one-night stands feel a little awkward afterwards and, if the couple meet up later for a date, may feel bashful about having been so sexual with a stranger.

This bashfulness is healthy; it indicates that the couple understand that sexuality is an important part of our humanity. It separates us from the animal kingdom and makes us more spiritual. The full-length mirror allows us to perceive ourselves as individuals with a unique consciousness and thus plays an important role in our sexual identity. We yearn to have sex, and to be known to our partners through the sexual experience. We long to feel loved by our partners, even if those partners are relative strangers. Sex makes us vulnerable, which can be difficult to manage, but the chemicals that are released during sex make sex very rewarding.

Mating and pair-bonding are essential components of sex. By eliminating the pair-bonding aspect of sex, we are unwittingly affecting how we perceive members of the opposite sex. By having orgasms with multiple partners at the same time, we are confusing the evolutionary process of mating. When we make sex purely recreational, and remove intimacy, vulnerability and, more importantly, respect from the equation, we debase our humanity and move closer to the animal kingdom.

When we engage in multiple sexual experiences with many people, at the same time, we are vulnerable. Women especially may be abused by this process. While many swinging clubs are strict in making men take a back seat until women initiate, this does not change the fact that when you are lying naked on a bed, surrounded by men, if one of them decides to touch you in an inappropriate way, what are you supposed to do? How many women feel comfortable standing up to the sexually inappropriate behaviour knowing that it will end the sex session for everyone given the awkwardness that would ensue? How many women clearly state before a swinging session begins the kind of sexual activities that they will and will not tolerate? How many men do?

The question that I am left with therefore is how do people make sense of themselves as sexual human beings when they experience the thrills of sexual chemistry and the highs of the dopamine reward system but have none of the emotional or psychological connections that make this behaviour safe for us in the first place?

We know that when men watch other people having sex it increases their sexual anxiety (mytonia) and tension. The only way that they can release this tension is through the orgasm, which is as powerful as heroin in terms of its ability to shut down all fear-based emotions. In the same way that heroin is addictive, so sex can be, too. It's quite plausible that swingers may have started out in the lifestyle full of fear and trepidation but having participated in their first orgy, and experienced an overload of dopamine, phenylethlamine, oxytocin and testosterone, become addicted to the experience to the detriment of regular loving intimacy with their partner.

If vasopressin makes men feel a sense of connection to their partners, and also a sense of loyalty and protection towards them, what happens to men when they have sex with ten different women at the same time? Where does that vasopressin response land, and with whom?

If a wife believes her husband has no particular bond with her, given how frequently he has sex with other women, does this make her feel more secure or insecure?

Swingers might not be aware that the brain is like the Grand Canyon. Let me explain. The Grand Canyon was forged millions of years ago by glacial waters that left the crevices and valleys that we see today. Imagine if there was another huge flood through the Grand Canyon for, let's say, 20 years. Eventually new valleys would be formed by the flowing water boring into the rock. The brain is similar: the more you engage in a particular behaviour, the deeper and stronger the valleys become. These new neural pathways replace what went before.

So if a couple previously gained sexual arousal from slow, sensual massage just with each other, once they start swinging, those erogenous zones will need to be stimulated in different ways and probably by more people to allow the couple to experience arousal. Only through abstinence from swinging will the couple regain their original sensual selves.

Having said all that, there must be some benefits to swinging or why else would hundreds of thousands of couples take part in it? Well, in terms of raising one's self-esteem, what could be better than being ravished by a roomful of strangers? If our sense of fear and anxiety disappears during orgasm and men feel huge surges of testosterone, i.e. power, from participating in group sex, then it can't be that hard to convince yourself that your life choice is a good one.

Interestingly, the kind of person that's aroused by sex with strangers is someone who may not have very particular tastes in others; if they did, then sexual desire would disappear the moment the bed was occupied by someone they didn't find attractive. This seldom happens, it seems.

David Schnarch, the sex therapist, believes we have three sexual thresholds: the emotional, physical and psychological. If we are in a bright room, we may be unable to become aroused if our preference is for dark environments. If we are in a dark room, but our partner has been critical of us, no amount of foreplay will arouse us.

It seems to me that swingers must have low arousal thresholds not to be affected by the amount of scenarios that can play out in any given session.

## WHY IS SEX SO MUCH FUN?

Sex is so much fun because, to put it bluntly, Gaia needs us to have lots of it to ensure our survival. The reason we want sex some days but not on others is more complex. You might not want sex because your wife was rude to you earlier that day, because you lost your wallet or because you looked in the mirror and didn't like what you saw. That's if you're a typical 50-year-old man; a 25-year-old man could experience the same three scenarios and go all night, regardless. Why so? Testosterone, that's why.

In their mid twenties, men experience a huge surge of testosterone, which can last well into their mid thirties. Testosterone fuels our sex drive. Around ovulation time, women become more interested in sex, also thanks to an increase in their testosterone levels. As we age, and testosterone diminishes, we may experience a decrease in sexual desire. But testosterone is only half the story.

We have noted that when men have sex, a chemical called vasopressin is released. In animals, vasopressin contributes to long-term pair-bonding. In humans it's the same: the more a man orgasms with the same woman, the stronger the bond. In other words, for men, sex really is love. In women, oxytocin is released in larger quantities than in men during orgasm, leading women to want to cuddle men after sex, the same men who at this point are sound asleep literally seconds later. Men do have oxytocin, too, just not in the same quantities. Oxytocin turns off the gorilla. What this means is that men lose all sense of fear and anxiety when they have an orgasm. It's also when they are most vulnerable to being attacked by the woman or another man. Sharon Stone caused many a man to shiver in *Basic Instinct* and while I don't want to spoil it for you if you haven't seen it, suffice to say that having an orgasm with her put the lead male actor very much in harm's way.

What is true love, then, if swinging isn't it? Is it monogamy? Is it undying loyalty and commitment to one another or is it more about friendship than anything else? Picture if you will an angelic being standing behind a bar serving cocktails, they can be male or female, the choice is yours. Now imagine you ask for a drink, something the angel thinks would be exactly what you need at that time. So they turn to the drinks cabinet and pull out large colourful crystal containers with the following names written on them: dopamine, adrenaline, testosterone, oestrogen, norepinephrine, serotonin, phenylethlamine and finally another odd-shaped jar labelled 'endogenous opiates'.

How would you feel if I told you that these chemicals were released in your brain during every relationship you've ever had? Would you be disappointed?

Some people are. They prefer to believe in fortune telling or predetermination to explain why any two people fall in love. I, on the other hand, believe that understanding some of the universe's mysteries shouldn't lessen our appreciation of them.

## What Is True Love?

Mortimer Adler asserted that 'Love consists in giving without getting in return; in giving what is not owed, what is not due the other. That's why true love is never based, as associations for utility or pleasure are, on a fair exchange.'

True love knows that feelings are only a tiny part of the picture. True love is the doing, the giving, the listening and the supporting that happens long after any chemically induced lust has left our brains.

True love is going the extra mile for your partner, even when you don't feel you want to. It is knowing when to listen, when to embrace and when to speak kind words. True love is the adventure ride in the fairground where you strap yourself in and hope for the best. True love is risky, but it's worth it. True love is awareness, breath and touch. True love is Mindful.

## MINDFULNESS: PART ONE

To become a better lover we don't have to skulk around sex shops looking awkwardly at sex toys, all we have to do is to become more 'mindful'. (Mindfulness will be explored more fully in Chapter 5.)

Mindfulness meditation has been found to improve couples' sex lives in the following ways:

1. Being 'present'. Being present is to be aware of your thoughts and feelings as they happen. Mindfulness helps you to be more present to yourself and your partner by increasing the size of your anterior insular, which helps us to perceive our bodily experiences.
2. Slowing down. By slowing sex down, we can really tune in more to our partner's thoughts and feelings during sex, rather than racing to the end to achieve an orgasm.
3. Train your mind. Invasive thoughts can creep in when you least want them, for example during foreplay. By learning to meditate you can focus your mind more clearly on the sensations you are experiencing rather than on your 'to do' list.
4. Getting in touch. Studies by researcher Lori Brotto at the University of British Columbia found that mindfulness meditation helped women become more aware of their body's sexual response, enjoy sex more and overcome sexual dysfunction.
5. Understanding sensations. Mindfulness helps you to focus on your breathing, your movement and your bodily reactions. When we have sex, we sometimes focus only on genitalia or erogenous zones, missing this vital connection with our breath. Breath work is a key feature of tantric sex and tantric sex is always good!

## ATTRACTION

When I worked as a dating coach in the early part of my career, radio chat-show hosts often asked me questions such as why do we fall in love with one person and not another? It was a great question. Yes, we need to find the person physically attractive, yes they need to come from the same socio-economic background, share the same religious ideals, possess relatively similar intellectual acumen and enjoy our humour, but there is more to attraction than just that.

Let me give you an example. One of my clients was raised by a mother who was continuously critical and unsupportive. Throughout her childhood, my client, Trisha, remembers very few occasions when her mother expressed love or affection to her. Instead she was demanding and overbearing, forcing Trisha to almost beg for affection at times.

Thirty years later, having long since moved out of her dysfunctional home, Trisha landed a great job in a law firm. There she met Nigel, a tall, rugged barrister whom she immediately fell in love with.

Three years after they married, when the love chemicals had worn off, Trisha started to notice that Nigel was critical of her, he was stand-offish and lacked warmth towards her. After a few sessions of therapy she was able to process the fact that she had unwittingly chosen a man with all the same characteristics as her mother. Why? Why do we choose to marry people who will treat us as badly as our parents might have?

Do you remember the toothbrush we mentioned earlier? If our most important habits are stored and processed in this brain area, such as cooking, eating, bathing, etc., we shouldn't be too surprised to learn that our emotional habits may also be stored there. We learn how to open up, how to trust, to be intimate or to hold back according to the way in which we were loved in our families.

Children who were parented properly and who have healthy brains tend to choose partners with equally healthy brains. The toothbrush stores what psychologist John Money referred to as our 'Love Maps' – the ways of interacting with our lovers that we learned from our families. Some psychologists estimate that 85 per cent of our personalities are formed by the time we are eight years old.

As George Santayana says, 'Those who cannot remember the past are doomed to repeat it.' What this means in practice is that the most significant relationships you have before you are eight years old tend to be replicated in your adult love relationships. Did you experience rejection from a caregiver? Were there many different people who cared for you? Did you lack consistency in your daily routines because of family circumstances? All these situations can affect who you choose to love as an adult and what you define as 'love' as in the first place.

# 5

# THE BRAIN AT WAR

The Neuroscience of Conflict

What Do All Arguments Have in Common?

Handy Hint from Brain Science

## MEET STEVE AND JANE

Besides being a psychotherapist working with couples in a small private practice, I also dabble a little in business. One of my businesses involves running courses preparing couples for marriage. This gives me a wonderful opportunity to see just how different men are from women. I'm the ultimate people-watcher, and unashamedly so.

At 10.50 a.m. on a Saturday, 15 to 20 couples stream into a hotel function room. Men sit down, look straight up, face front and wait for the course to start. Women sit down, check their handbags, remove their coats, put back on their coats, check their handbags again, and look around.

Next I watch each individual couple more closely. She will usually start chatting first, touch his arm, smile at him, turn towards him, lean forward to get his attention, check to see where he's looking, ask him if he's nervous, will say if she is, etc. Meanwhile he's staring at his smartphone.

That for me sums up the difference between men and women. Women want to connect, men want to disconnect. Throughout the marriage course, we allude to this fact and how it can cause trouble in any marriage. A stay-at-home mother who yearns for adult company will crave attention, affection and stimulation from her just-in-the-door husband; he just wants to be left alone. So then we have a conversation that may go something like this:

> Steve: Hey, how are you?
> Jane: I'm good, tired but good.
> S: How was your day? Were you busy, the kids behave themselves?
> J: Ah, they were okay, the usual chaos. How did the meeting go with the new client? Were you happy with it?
> S: Yeah, it was fine. What's for dinner?
> J: I was thinking of cooking fish, is that okay?
> S: Yeah, I suppose, if there's nothing else.

He leaves the kitchen to go to the sitting room, turns on the TV and brings the kids with him, leaving her to cook.

What do you think we would discover if we could see this couple's thoughts as well as hear their words? Let's imagine we can. It might go something like this:

> Steve: Hey, how are you? – *I want to know how Jane is.*
> Jane: I'm good, tired but good – *I hope he sees how tired I am. I want a back rub. I'm bored out of my mind. My mind is numb. I'm sick of screaming kids and breaking up fights, why does he get to go to work when I have to stay here?*
> S: How was your day? Were you busy, the kids behave themselves? – *I want to know how Jane and the kids are.*
> J: Ah, they were okay, the usual chaos. How did the meeting go with the new client? Were you happy with it? – *Bloody typical, nothing, no appreciation, no affection, nothing. Why hasn't he noticed that scratch under my eye from our 3-year-old tearing at my face, does he not see it, does he see it but not care, does he not find me attractive enough to notice these things any more?*
> S: Yeah, it was fine. What's for dinner? – *I would like to know what we are having for dinner.*

J: I was thinking of cooking fish, is that okay? – *Did that just happen, all he cares about is what he's getting for dinner, oh my God, what's wrong with me, why do I tolerate this?*
S: Yeah, I suppose, if there's nothing else. – *I am not a fan of fish, but I'm hungry so I suppose that will have to do.*

At this point the scene is set for an explosive argument. At no point will Steve have a clue what's really going on. While sitting in bed together later he might innocently ask: 'What time are you going to your parents on Saturday?'

Having been angry and frustrated since he arrived home, she may reply with seething contempt with something like, 'What do you care?' You can imagine where the conversation goes from there.

## THE NEUROSCIENCE OF CONFLICT

To see how the brain works in practice, let's analyse what happened between Steve and Jane. Bear in mind that this exchange may have only taken about ten seconds and you will come to appreciate how amazingly complex we human beings really are.

Steve enters the kitchen and they see each other for the first time that day. Their visual cortices are activated. Jane scans all over Steve's face to see what she can tell about his mood, his stress levels and whether or not he's happy to see her. Steve just sees Jane and the kids.

Jane's gorilla activates when she senses that Steve is not as happy to see her as she is to him. This is a misperception in Jane caused by insecurity learned when she was a child. When her dad came home from work, he was never affectionate with Jane's mum but instead was quite abrupt with her and his children, including Jane. A chemical called cortisol now floods over Jane's neural pathways, increasing her heart rate and preparing her for a fight.

Jane's long-term memories, which are stored in the USB stick, start to colour her perception of reality and she begins to feel once more like she is a frightened child. This all happens beyond her awareness in her subconscious. Now Jane has to work hard to prevent her insecurities from spilling out so her glucose levels start to drop. She needs willpower to maintain a cool head as she chats to Steve. Willpower, we now know, uses up glucose, and doesn't last long.

For Steve, being tired and hungry, his thermostat is in overdrive. His adrenal glands are activated, telling him that if he does not quickly replenish his body with the fuel it needs, he will not be able to function as a father to the two expectant children who crave his attention. Steve remembers what life was like when his mother, who worked outside the home, was seldom there when his father returned from work, leaving Steve and his sister to fend for themselves. Symbolically having a meal cooked for him and his children tells Steve that all is okay in his world. Dinner is much more than a meal; it is a primitive symbol of being in a happy marriage.

As Jane's insecurities continue to grow during the exchange, she feels herself becoming angry. Adrenaline starts to flow through her blood vessels, sending messages to every part of her body. Her body stiffens in preparation for the oncoming stressful interchange that she believes may manifest at any second. The inner Sherlock is very active here, it controls her ability to think rationally and to process rewards from her environment. Where is the reward from Steve, where is the recognition she needs, or the appreciation? The ACC also recognises when we are in conflict, either with ourselves or with someone else. Her brain clouds over in a fog of confusion as more neurotransmitters send electrical impulses shooting up and down her spine, readying her for attack or, alternatively, for withdrawal from the conflict. Her professor shuts down at this point; it controls logical thinking. Logic seems far away right now. Meanwhile Steve is still hungry.

As Steve moves to the sitting room, Jane feels abandoned. Even more cortisol floods her brain so dinner is a quiet affair. Steve enjoys the quiet after his busy day; Jane, however, sees it as even more proof of their unsuitability for a life of raising children together. Dinner time in her family was a sombre affair; her distant father would scarcely acknowledge her mother's attempts to chat to him about her day, leaving Jane full of resentment and bitterness towards her dad. Here was Steve doing exactly that to her. What has she done to deserve this?

Jane is not feeling well. Her immune system is weak and she gets sick often. The stress caused by her arguments with Steve leads to the creation of a protein called calcitonin gene-related peptide or CGRP. This protein binds itself to other cells, making the prevention of illness even harder. Being unwell makes processing the argument more problematic. Stress begets stress.

Jane's inner Sherlock is always on alert trying to find proof that there is a conflict between what she is experiencing and what she is feeling. The inner Sherlock is an internal monitor. It allows us to change gears and move from one emotional state to another. Flexibility, which is essential for a healthy mind or relationship, is dependent on a functioning inner Sherlock. When it's working properly, people tend to be more easy-going, less stressed, less rigid and more open to going with the flow. People with high inner Sherlock activity tend to be obsessive and struggle with control.

To cope with the stress she feels, Jane's HPA system now takes over, sending messages to her brain, helping her to remember this experience for the future by encoding the memory. Her frontal lobe shuts down, making speech, concentration and appetite almost impossible. The HPA system reacts to perceived lack of control, feelings of uncertainty, unfairness and a lack of connection between people. This short interchange over dinner managed to invoke all four experiences for Jane and she stopped talking as a result.

During emotional outbursts, a group of chemicals called glucocorticoids are released, which break down neurons in the USB stick. This is bad news for encoding memories. Jane will not remember this argument as it happened but may only remember the emotional impact she perceives, which will be one of hurt and pain. Steve will have no awareness she feels this way.

Jane hadn't slept the night before this argument took place. Their 5-year-old had kept her awake, coughing in the room beside her. Without sufficient sleep, Jane had low levels of GABA, a chemical compound that regulates mood and peace of mind. Another chemical called glutamate is also affected by a lack of sleep. In this case Jane will find it difficult to process the conversation with Steve, see it for what it really is and not take it personally. Glutamate has a role in critical thinking and without it we may end up thinking irrationally but never knowing why.

So what if Jane and Steve go to therapy? Well, the conversation may go something like this:

Therapist: How can I help you both?

Jane: Steve doesn't care about me or the children.

Steve (reacts defensively): Of course I do, how dare you say that.

J: Well you never show it, you never show me that you care about me.

S: What are you talking about?

T: Jane, can you give me an example of how you think Steve doesn't care about you?

At this point Jane recalls the earlier argument and repeats it verbatim.

Sometimes a therapist will then say something like this: 'Steve, is what Jane said true? Did you come home from work and just wonder what was for dinner? Is it possible that this was a little insensitive to Jane? Does Jane deserve a bit more from you than that?'

It seems that this therapist has gone on the wrong tangent in attributing the blame to Steve for the couple's difficulty. A brain-wise therapist would take a completely different approach. They might say something like this: 'Jane, when Steve came home from work and walked into the kitchen, what were you feeling and what were you expecting from him at that point?'

Then the therapist may ask questions such as: 'Jane, when you were a child and your dad came home, what used to happen? How did he interact with you or your mum?' The brain-wise therapist does the same with Steve and then helps the couple to track their interaction minute by minute. What I do with my clients is explain the way their brains were working during the argument and how sometimes our brains can get us into trouble.

To resolve this issue, Jane and Steve need to know how to let their brains cool off. They can do this by assessing if they are stressed. Some questions they should consider asking themselves are:

- How am I feeling right now?
- How is my partner feeling?
- Is what I am feeling an accurate reflection of what's happening?
- Is there anything I can do to bring a sense of calm to the discussion?

Steve and Jane have slightly different brains. While Jane's is smaller than Steve's, she has a better ability to use language than Steve does. During the argument both adrenaline and cortisol were released in their brains. This makes Steve's brain agitated, which he will try to relieve by debating with Jane. She sees this as defensiveness and a denial of responsibility on his part. The female brain is wired differently. She remembers everything he says during the row and wants to talk it through. This helps her brain to release oxytocin and serotonin. Serotonin is helpful in quietening her inner Sherlock. The oxytocin makes her feel closer to Steve.

If this couple can stop talking at each other, and take a moment to drink a cup of coffee or tea together, their brains will have the space they need to reflect and pause. Researchers have found that couples tend to rate each other as more friendly when they share warm drinks.

Novelty is a key ingredient in conflict resolution. Doing new things together increases the physical size of the USB stick, which is good for managing our emotions. Staying up all night arguing in the same room is not a good idea. Getting out of the house and doing something different together is a much better to way to heal from an emotional upheaval.

If this couple can visualise a positive reward for resolving the argument, such as going to the cinema, making love, or eating a nice dinner, it will activate the ventral tegmental area of their brains, which processes rewards. This will give them both a shot of dopamine, which will elevate their mood and create a desire to reconnect.

The toothbrush can be motivated towards new behaviours if they both make a conscious decision and use their professors to change how they interact during arguments. This will involve sitting down afterwards and reflecting on how they want rows to be resolved in future. For example, they may decide the following:

- We are not allowed to name-call.
- We must agree to take turns when we are speaking.
- It's not okay to walk away.
- Sneering is unhelpful.
- We must maintain good eye contact.

To cool off their brains, this couple could go for a walk or engage in gentle exercise together. This will stimulate the release of opioids, which can make them both feel better. However, it's important that they aren't angry when they leave the house. Studies in Yale University from the 1990s found that the subject's state of mind played a role in whether the exercise they took had a calming effect. If they exercised while angry, their physiological condition worsened. We don't want that to happen to Jane and Steve; they're in enough trouble already.

Jane has a conflict of interest. She wants to honour her childhood memories but at the same time she wants to reconnect with Steve. She thinks that she is being logical in her argument but this is not how the brain works. Our feelings impact on our thinking more than we can know. Jane is no different.

Jane is stuck because she feels rewarded by sticking to her position. As far as she is concerned, she is right and her perception of the row with Steve is accurate, so she gets to feel smug. This triggers her reward centres and releases dopamine. However, it also prevents her from imagining the reward she would get from calming down and maybe being affectionate with Steve. She needs to be reminded that there are two reward centres to consider, Steve's and hers.

Jane trusts her memories. She believes they are accurate. She is combining memories of hurt and abandonment from the past with her perception of how she is being treated today. This is also a mistake. Her brain-wise therapist will remind Jane that memories are not always that accurate, and that checking in to reality as it is happening today is a far better way to prevent an argument from spiralling out of control. To do this she needs to ask Steve if her perception is indeed correct.

## What Do All Arguments Have in Common?

We only really argue when we feel threatened. If we feel we're being disrespected or not listened to, it causes us to react negatively. The gorilla has several responses it can give to feeling threatened. It can make us fight, freeze or flee. It doesn't matter if the argument is over money, sex or parenting, the one common feature that makes us all defensive or angry is when we believe that we are being threatened in some way. Yet when our gorilla springs to life it's very difficult to stand still and chat rationally about the issue.

At this point you might have stormed away, begun to stonewall or become flooded with cortisol to such a point that you are unable to respond in a meaningful way to the conversation. The psychologist John Gottman calls these 'marriage busters', more specifically: contempt, criticism, stonewalling and defensiveness. Each of these behaviours is an external response to the internal threat that is being assessed, correctly or incorrectly, by your gorilla. The solution is to give each other time to let your brains cool down. Walk away. This is essential if you want to find a resolution.

## Handy Hint from Brain Science

The old saying 'Don't go to bed angry' needs to be consigned to the history bin. If they are in conflict, one of the most important things a couple can do is to get adequate sleep. Sleep restores the chemical balance in your brain, which is vital if you want your professor to take over and help you both solve the problem in hand.

Remember, arguments are a normal, healthy part of any relationship. But you can help your relationship along nicely if you abide by the following golden rules:

- Never argue in front of other people as it leaves you both feeling more vulnerable.
- Don't name-call or use sarcasm to express your frustration or anger.
- Only discuss one issue at a time.
- Give each other as much time as you need to calm down, even while arguing.
- Shouting matches are a bad idea, especially if there are children present.
- Learn to observe and read each other's body language better.
- Can you read each other's body language when you are anxious, angry or afraid?
- Physical affection deactivates your gorilla and lets your professor take over.
- Write down the most important aspects of the row and share them someplace outside the house or apartment.
- Try the pen trick, which causes you both to smile. If nothing else, you will both look silly, which will ease the tension between you.
- Finally, don't be afraid to discuss what needs to be discussed. Remember Carl Jung: 'What you resist persists.'

## Handy Hint from Brain Science

If you are feeling guilty or ashamed after an argument – wash your hands. We now know that by washing our hands we are psychologically cleansing the unpleasant emotions we feel. Researchers had subjects remember a time when they behaved 'immorally' or shamefully, then had them clean their hands with an antiseptic wipe. Then they asked the subjects to rate their levels of guilt after wiping their hands. Each felt significantly less guilty. This stuff really works!

Finally, use the 'as if' principle to restore peace in the relationship. To do this you each need to act as if you are calm, as if you have forgiven each other and as if you feel connected once more. This behaviour tricks the brain into believing that order has been restored, and lets you get on with the business of loving each other.

# 6

# A QUICK GUIDE TO THE BRAIN:
## PART TWO

Where Is Rejection Felt in the Brain?

The Ultimatum Game

What Is 'Gut Instinct'?

## How Can Better Knowing Your Brain Help Your Marriage?

In my opinion, brain science is amazing. Every day it's revealing more to us about why we behave the way we do. For understanding relationships, brain science has a number of very practical uses:

- As a way for couples to process difficult emotions
- As a source of hope when couples feel stuck
- It can debunk myths about change and habits
- Brain science has insights into why we argue
- Couples can learn to communicate more effectively
- It can reduce stress, both internal and external
- Brain science helps couples reconnect
- It can show us how to maintain love, long after the lust has faded
- We can overcome anxiety and fear by using simple brain-science principles
- Finally, it shows us how to tap into our unconscious wisdom

No matter what the issue, and believe me I have heard many different issues in my practice, each and every one can be solved by brain science. Of this I have no doubt.

The majority of difficulties I work with centre around one person's attitude to another person's behaviour, such as:

- He doesn't support me enough
- She is lazy
- She never wants sex
- He won't spend time with the kids
- She flies off the handle for no reason
- He criticises me all the time

In the majority of cases, when I look hard enough, I can find one or more brain parts not doing their job adequately. My job, then, is to assess which brain parts should be worked on and which interventions should be made to produce the desired change.

Couples come to marriage with some ingrained beliefs about their partner and themselves. These may include ideas such as:

- That's just the way I am (I can't change)
- That's just how he is (he will never change)
- Emotions are reality
- Memories are facts
- My perception of past events is accurate
- I am right, so he must be wrong
- Arguments are opportunities to prove you're right
- The past is the past, no point talking about it now
- My gut instinct is always right

We find change difficult in relationships because we believe that giving up our need to be right will leave us worse off. Nothing could be further from the truth. When we develop an attitude of openness and flexibility, we strengthen our brain connections and teach our brains new ways of relating to others. When we can let go of our problems, the orbitofrontal cortex is activated. This governs our ability to move our attention from one issue to the other. If

Jane, our fictional subject, can finally move past her need to be right, then she and Steve have a real chance of moving forward.

Jane is overcome with fear. This inhibits logical thinking as the gorilla has control here instead. Many of us share similar fears to Jane. Fears like 'Am I lovable?' or 'How will I survive if this marriage doesn't work out?' Such fear keeps us stuck, perhaps in relationships that are not good for us. Fear prevents us from building our relationships into something great. Fear stops us from seeing the positive results that can come from addressing the problems we know exist in the relationship. Fear prevents change.

If your partner is in a negative state of mind, it might be better for you to give them space. As social human beings, we're all influenced by the feeling states of those around us.

Think of the last time you attended a meeting where one person looked nervous or anxious. Within minutes everybody else in the room probably felt the same way. Fear and anger are contagious.

The same thing happens at home. Then we get confused. We sense our partner's fear or anger but don't quite know what to do about it. We may internalise it at this point and think it's our fault. An argument will probably ensue. The solution here is to walk away and give each other space. For women this can be difficult: most women are problem-solvers. They see their partner is quiet, they realise that he's stressed and they believe that if only he chatted about his stress, *then* he would be okay.

This is the opposite of how many men process stress. Men need to be left alone. They do not in general like to be asked to 'get in touch' with their emotions, not by their partners or by therapists. Men know what they are feeling as much as women do, they just tend to avoid discussing it. To avoid serious conflict with a stressed partner or husband, leave him alone until he initiates a conversation.

## HOW DO WE KNOW IF OUR GORILLA IS ON THE LOOSE?

If we feel a sense of dread but don't know why, our gorilla may be to blame. If we feel we are better off being by ourselves, it might be a fear response that's hidden from our conscious brain. If we have an overall sense of anger but don't know why, it may be a result of the way the gorilla is trying to process the intense feelings it's creating. Finally, when you hear yourself express something like, 'Oh, things will never change between us,' such statements of negativity can be rooted in an overactive gorilla.

## WHERE IS REJECTION FELT IN THE BRAIN?

Researchers have conducted experiments measuring pain. They have found that when subjects directed their attention to the pain being administered in the experiment, they rated that pain as more intense than when they distracted themselves away from the same pain. In other words, if a couple comes for therapy to discuss their problems, and all they focus on is the pain in their relationship, then they will feel the marriage is in a worse state than perhaps it is. Distraction may be a clinical tool after all.

Jane is feeling rejection from being alone with the children all day. She feels cut off from her friends and family. She misses going for nice long lunches with her best friend and she especially misses her work colleagues. She was popular at work and was secretary of the social committee. A 'social butterfly' is how she used to describe herself.

New research by Dr Giorgia Silani in Italy has found that the experience of social rejection is the same as if Jane was feeling actual physical pain. Silani explains that her data shows that when we experience social discomfort or 'social pain', there is activation in an area of the brain where it is traditionally believed physical pain is processed, what she terms the 'posterior' full-length mirror. This happens whether the pain is experienced directly or vicariously.

So, unbeknown to Jane, her brain is telling her that she is in physical pain. It's no wonder that Steve's lack of consideration was so hurtful. Jane needed a loving, warm embrace from Steve when he came home. Instead she received little more than a passing interest in how her day had been. Physical affection here could have gone a long way to ease Jane's pain.

Naomi Eisenberger and her colleague Matthew Lieberman created a clever but simple game to test for social pain called 'Cyberball'. In the game, subjects played a computerised version of catch with two other players. The two other players were actually the computer. The subject was wired to our trusty fMRI machine while they played. During the game at a random time, the other two 'players' would suddenly exclude the test subject. The inner Sherlock activated immediately. This is what the two researchers were measuring. The same brain part that measured physical pain also registered emotional pain or rejection.

The next stage of the study was to test how best to treat this social pain. Lieberman had a theory that if social pain registered in the same brain part as rejection, and we could treat physical pain with common painkillers, like Tylenol, would this simple medication work on social pain in the same way?

He recruited two groups of volunteers. Each subject had suffered a significant relationship breakdown in the previous weeks and was indeed feeling rejection. To test his theory, he created a control group who were given a placebo, and the main group who were given Tylenol. Each subject was asked to write a diary of the level of rejection they felt each night before going to bed. After two weeks the Tylenol group reported significantly less pain than the placebo group. To Lieberman it proved that the cure for heartbreak wasn't buckets of ice cream, but two simple painkillers, twice a day. Heartbreak is real, but heartbreak is also curable.

When we argue with our families, or have a serious falling out with our lovers, the feelings that arise in us can be experienced as a very real form of physical pain. At least now we know that we don't have to suffer indefinitely.

Jane and Steve need something to look forward to, like a night away in a hotel or a meal out with friends. This would give them both a reward and would make the sacrifices they are making seem worthwhile. Getting social support and widening out the solutions to include other people are the best ways they can restore the love they once felt. When they are both depleted and exhausted, and have nothing left to give, being loving to each other can seem altogether too much.

Steve worries too much and too often. He worries if they will have enough money to pay the mortgage each month. This worry affects how his brain processes information. It slows down information going from the right side of his brain to the left side. This means that he is unable to take the steps he needs to fix the problem, like working more efficiently, changing jobs or buying a smaller house. Instead he is too caught up in himself to be able to offer Jane the support she needs.

This couple needs a healthy dose of optimism. Optimism offers its own reward. It tells us that all will be well in our world, that we have everything under control and that we can manage. It gives us a sense of security. In order for our brains to function fully, we need to allow ourselves to feel optimistic. The journal *Psychology Today* has reported that our inner Sherlock works with our gorilla to downplay negative emotional responses and helps us picture future events by recalling how we felt about similar events in the past.

Working with a brain-wise therapist, this couple might be asked some of the following questions:

- What would your ideal future look like? Think of next week, next month, and next year.
- What did you do well in the past that helped you both overcome the issues in the relationship?
- Let's imagine you have reached the goal of a happy, satisfactory relationship. What is different now? What do you notice most?
- If a miracle happened overnight, and everything was better in your relationship, what is the first thing that you would notice, and who would notice it first?

These questions can help Jane and Steve turn their attention to the future, and allow them to imagine life free from their current problems. This is one of the best ways to become 'unstuck'. Helping the couple to feel good about their future will also allow them to be more imaginative in finding ways to resolve their problems.

Every argument we have activates more or less the same brain regions. Now that we know how to manage each brain region, all we need to do (which is the challenge) is to actively work together to quieten the various brain parts that are triggered when we fight.

### Handy Hint from Brain Science

One thing to remember when you are angry with your partner is that the worst thing you can do is to take out your anger on them. It was once believed that 'venting' is an important part of resolving conflict. We have since discovered, thanks to fMRI machines, that this is a huge mistake. Venting just makes you angrier, it does not reduce the emotional intensity around what you are angry about.

## MINDFULNESS: PART TWO

One of the most important interventions that this couple can make to help their relationship is to practise mindfulness. This is the exercise of bringing our attention to ourselves and focusing on what we are feeling and thinking at any given time. Mindfulness is an adaptation of Buddhist meditation, but it's more easily practised than the form Buddhists use.

Millions of people are using mindfulness to ease tension and reduce stress. When couples practise it together they can share simple exercises like the three-minute breathing space. This can be done while they are trying to cool off their brains. Taking three minutes away from each other while focusing on their breathing is a great way to gain the space they need to prepare their brains to communicate more effectively.

There is conclusive evidence that mindfulness can improve the quality of your life. It affects the following areas: the gorilla, the HPA axis, the full-length mirror and the autonomic nervous system; it reduces the production of stress hormones like cortisol and it quietens the inner Sherlock.

Brain-wave activity changes when we practise mindfulness. We learn to think more clearly, calm ourselves more quickly from states of stress and develop insight into how to solve problems more effectively.

## THE ROLE OF COMPASSION

Can we ever have too much compassion in our relationships? I don't think so. Being compassionate allows us to be more thoughtful, forgiving and sensitive to the needs of others. We associate a lack of compassion with a person who is hard, cruel and inhumane. In my experience, couples in conflict find it very hard to be compassionate, either with themselves or each other.

Studies have shown that compassion is registered in the insular and cingulate cortex. When we meditate we increase activation in these areas, meaning we are more likely to be compassionate towards others. We know that not being aware of our own feelings makes us much less likely to be aware of others' feelings. So start with yourself.

Compassion is an attitude we need to adopt. It's a state of mind. It activates our empathy neurons and makes us more enjoyable to be around. By being tuned into our partners' feelings we can better understand how they might need us in that moment. In the process, we will be perceived as more trustworthy and less threatening. This will quieten their gorilla and increase activity in their mirror neurons. Mirror neurons are found all over the brain and allow us to mimic what we see, to feel what others are feeling and to tune into our partners' state of mind at any given time.

## DEVELOPING EMOTIONAL INTELLIGENCE

Daniel Goleman popularised the term 'emotional intelligence' in 1995. The concept had first been explored by psychologists Peter Salovey and John Mayer. It refers to the ability to recognise our feelings and those of others and to behave in an appropriate manner in accordance with what we discern. Goleman outlined five key aspects of emotional intelligence: empathy, attunement, empathic accuracy, social cognition and social facility.

A number of years ago we were discussing feelings and thoughts in one of my marriage seminars. One woman piped up that as far as she was concerned, 'His job is to know what I'm thinking, without me having to tell him.' We all laughed. We thought she was joking. She wasn't. She was deadly serious. That's taking emotional intelligence to a whole new level.

We need to practise trying to read our partners' moods and emotions. It can be a good exercise to 'check in' regularly and ask, 'What's going on for you at the moment?' Then compare this with what we thought they were feeling. It can be surprising to learn that we are so far off the mark.

## FAIRNESS

Fairness, as a theme, crops up regularly in my therapy sessions. Take Dale and Emma, for example. Emma complained that it was she who had to get up every night to feed their twins. Dale slept soundly each night, even on weekends. I was amazed she had tolerated his laziness for so long. In the session, she defended him by saying how hard he worked at his own business. However, reading her body language (eye rolling and sneering) I believed that despite what she was saying, she felt resentment for him deep down.

In the next session I asked to speak to her on her own. I was told that not only did he sleep through the night, but every Friday he went drinking with his friends and most of Saturday was spent in bed, sleeping off his hangover. His poor children rarely saw him as a result. This wasn't fair on anybody. Emma now realised that Dale wasn't lazy, he was an alcoholic.

Jane felt the same as Emma. She didn't think that Steve's workload was as much as hers or that he spent as much time with his children as he should have. Steve also drank too much, leaving Jane feeling uncertain about the future of the relationship. Fairness is a key ingredient for a happy marriage, and for stable brain functioning.

## THE ULTIMATUM GAME

Since 1982, social scientists have used a game called the 'Ultimatum Game' to monitor how people respond to fairness. The game goes as follows. The first player is given a sum of money, say €100. All the player has to do is to propose to the second player how this money should be split between them. If player two agrees with the proposed split, then both players keep the money and everyone is happy. If player two rejects the offer then neither player gets anything. What a great game.

Alan Sanfey of the Donders Centre for Cognitive Neuroimaging in the Netherlands has studied the brains of people playing this game. When a proposal is made by player one that is deemed unfair by player two, there is activity in the dorsolateral professor and the anterior insular of player two. In other words, fairness is perceived in the brain. But fairness is individualistic. What one player might accept as fair another might reject as unfair.

This situation is played out in our relationships every day without us even knowing. Some people call it scorekeeping. So you might hear yourself think, 'He went to the supermarket, bought the shopping and cooked dinner, therefore it's fair if I mind the kids tomorrow while he watches the match.' By maintaining a good proportion of fairness in your relationship you are much more likely to feel satisfied. Marriage expert John Gottman calls these act of kindness 'love deposits'. Our aim is to have a bigger balance of deposits in our partner's bank, or roughly the same in both banks, if at all possible. When fairness gets kicked out of sync we might resort to punishing our partner. But why punish anyone; what's the benefit to us?

Punishing our partner for transgressing our written or unwritten rules can feel satisfying. The part of the brain involved in doing this is called the dorsal reward centre and it releases a sort of reward in our brains when we believe that we have punished our partner to the right amount. Too much of a punishment leaves us feeling guilty, but just the right amount, well, that's very satisfying. All of this makes working with couples challenging. They may be enjoying the punishments they are doling out to each other and not want to stop.

## WHAT IS 'GUT INSTINCT'?

Cooperation is a cornerstone for success in life. We need to cooperate with others to survive. We need to cooperate with our husbands and wives to enjoy stable marriages. When we do something nice for them like giving a back rub, preparing a nice meal, anything altruistic, unconsciously we expect something back in return. That's understandable. We are only human. If we don't get anything back in return, the left USB stick and anterior insular light up in our brains.

The anterior insular or full-length mirror is the part of yourself you know as your 'gut instinct'. This gives you feedback at an unconscious level and in this case it tells you that being so loving and so kind is not a good idea. You're not going to get anything back in return. The USB stick has a role in memory formation so what's happening here is your brain is telling you to remember that being this kind or loving is a waste of your time. This is why we have a nagging feeling deep down when we feel taken for granted; your brain doesn't like when you're being used.

## REKINDLING TRUST AFTER A CONFLICT

We all know how raw we feel after an argument. There may have been tears, harsh words and raised voices. How do we rekindle trust when this happens? Brain science is shedding some light on this important question.

Trust has a chemical basis: oxytocin. Also called 'the cuddle chemical', oxytocin is released in our brains when we feel a strong bond with someone. When we embrace, shake hands or kiss each other, oxytocin is released, making us feel more connected to one another. Paul J. Zak is the expert in this area and he has conducted years of research into how we can learn to trust each other more. He has concluded that the more physical affection there is between couples, the more they will trust each other. So get hugging and kissing as much as possible.

However, Zak has recently discovered that oxytocin has a second purpose, not nearly as pleasurable. When we argue with our lovers and feel upset, the argument activates the lateral septum, which has a key role in managing anxiety. The lateral septum has recently been found to attach to other important brain regions that manage anxiety. At this point, oxytocin intensifies the anxious feelings, making us feel even worse. This can put us on edge and make us more fearful of confrontations in the future. So we end up in an ever-increasing cycle of fear, argument, stress and avoidance. Not good.

When there is a breach of trust, the inner Sherlock activates the gorilla. This then communicates with the reward centres in your brain to tell them no reward is coming. They then inform the motor centres that control your behaviour that you need to act on this information. As a result, you behave like someone who has been hurt by the breakdown in trust. You might be angry, cry or retaliate depending on your personal temperament or how you feel at that point.

Some men aren't trusted by their partners. She may have found an inappropriate email on his laptop, and so she confronts him. If he is innocent, his brain will respond and produce a hormone called dihydrotestosterone (DHT). It's been found that increased levels of DHT increase the desire for physical confrontation so my advice is be slow to accuse someone of an affair, until you have all the facts, at least. If he's guilty, well, that's a different story.

The way to increase trust between you is to tell each other that you trust each other. It's that simple. This will lead to the production of oxytocin, which in turn will make you behave more trustworthily.

## The Role of Laughter after a Conflict

It's been said that the shortest distance between two people is a smile, but actually it's laughter. In the 2014 'Society for Neuroscience' newsletter, it was reported that 'More recent imaging studies examining the brains of healthy people show that while motor and reward pathways in the brain are primarily activated when we laugh, the anterior cingulate, a brain region involved in conflict detection, is also engaged when people are presented with something humorous.'

This region is not only involved in 'getting' jokes but is also essential for 'coping with difficult feelings or emotions or even social situations', explains Scott Weems, a cognitive neuroscientist at the University of Maryland.

So rather than just going for a nice meal together to heal after an argument, watch a comedy DVD or go to your nearest comedy club. You can never have enough laughter in your relationship, a bit like sex.

## The Power of Persuasion

Power is very important in helping us feel that we are in control. Knowing that we can get our needs met through persuasion reassures us that this relationship is a good one and worthy of our time and effort.

Persuasion has been studied with fascinating results. The Asch Experiment is one such study. Subjects were brought to a room along with five other people. The other five subjects were working with the researcher. They were asked to give their views on the length of a number of black lines on large white cards. They all did so and nothing unusual happened. Then they were all tested again and this time the confederates lied about which line was longest and they all said that one particular line was longer than the other, when it clearly wasn't. In almost every case where this happened, the test subject agreed with the confederates and gave the incorrect answer. They literally changed their perception of reality to keep in with the group.

G.R. Miller defined persuasive communication as 'any message that is intended to shape, reinforce or change the responses of others' (Miller, p. 11). When we can influence our partner to do what we need or want, we feel better about ourselves. In the brain there is increased activity in the temporal sulcus. Persuasion is a positive dimension of relationships and happy couples have figured out how best to manipulate (I mean work with) their partner so that both feel satisfied with the outcomes of their transactions.

In summary, follow these basic steps for a trouble-free relationship:

- Try to ground yourself in reality, not just in your own perspective of the issue.
- Assess your feelings for accuracy, they might be misleading you.
- Take a long-term time perspective.
- Always look for the rewards that may come from resolving the problem.
- Use novelty and laughter to repair any damage done from the row.
- Learn to say nothing, stop nagging and appreciate each other more.
- Allow each other a reasonable amount of influence in the relationship.
- See the argument from your partner's perspective and assess it in that light.
- Aim for compromise at all times.
- Never seek to be 'right' during a conflict, this just damages the other's sense of self.

# 7

## WHAT'S INSIDE YOUR BRAIN?

Harry's Monkeys

When Two Brains Go to a Wedding

The Amygdala or Gorilla

## A Neuron

The most basic cell in the brain is called a neuron. Electricity flows through neurons and gives life to the brain. Neurons have two parts, the nucleus and cytoplasm, the fluid that encapsulates it. Protruding from the neuron is a projection called an axon, which is used for sending electrical transmissions, and a dendrite, which receives them.

A young adult has about ten billion neurons in their brain. We also have a further hundred billion support cells that hold the neurons together, assist in the growth of the neurons and are responsible for removing waste when the neuron dies. Blood vessels keep the brain alive and link all the neurons and support cells.

In order to communicate with each other, neurons need connections that transmit electrical signals from one to another. There are minute gaps between the neurons known as synapses. To carry the signal through the gap or synapse, there are many different types of chemicals called neurotransmitters. These bring the signals by osmosis into the neurons.

Synapses are not permanent fixtures in your brain; if they are not used they will wither and die. If you strapped your left arm behind your back for ten years, when you remove the strapping, you might discover that moving your left arm is almost impossible. If you don't use it, you lose it.

According to Louis Cozolino, neurons are able to change who we are by communicating 'across the synapse which changes the internal biochemistry of the cell which in turn activates the mRNA (messenger ribonucleic acid, the material that translates the protein into new brain structure) and protein synthesis to change cellular structure' (Cozolino, p. 5).

This sounds complicated but in essence some brain cells make new cells with different functions depending on the messages they are given. When I share a moment of loving tenderness with a partner, I am essentially growing a different brain area at that point and repeated actions such as caressing their face will strengthen the connections between the cells. This is how love or tenderness can 'grow' within us.

Alternatively, once we engage in an activity or become involved in an experience, horse riding for example, new neurons will grow in the brain in order to manage, remember and facilitate that experience. Doing the same activity repeatedly makes the connections thicker between the neurons. So if you think about smokers, for example, the more they smoke, the thicker the connections become that move nicotine throughout the blood vessels. It also sends signals to their brains to increase their heart rate and lung movement.

One aspect that I personally love about the brain, which I wish more people were aware of, is the fact that neurons form over one hundred trillion connections with each other! This is more than all the Internet connections in the world. Try this awareness exercise if you can, just to get grounded. Touch your forehead for ten seconds with your hand. Now gradually become aware that inside your head lies the most complex living organism in the known universe. This organism can change the destiny of the world. It can save hundreds of thousands of lives. It can build monuments, learn languages, make music and even create life. How cool is that?

To add to this magnificence, neuroscientists have recently discovered that the brain is not a *tabula rasa* as Aristotle asserted but has a feature we call 'plasticity'. Plasticity means that the brain can grow new neural connections (neurogenesis) and therefore can learn new behaviours, skills, attitudes and activities. At 42 years of age, I have begun learning Spanish so I can teach it to my daughter. Before I knew about plasticity I believed such a project was useless, that my language acquisition skills died after my final state exams. Now I'm finding it both easy and satisfying.

The plasticity of the brain is what ensures our survival. Being able to adapt to new relationships and learn new activities guarantees that we have a chance to continue our species. We can gain confidence, go from being geek to goddess, or develop public-speaking skills that we never thought possible. None of this could happen without plasticity. In fact, no one could ever get remarried after a death or divorce without plasticity. We would be too stuck in the habits of our previous relationship to learn the new behaviours needed to make the second relationship work.

Governing the functions of our neurons, synapses and dendrites are the major brain areas listed below. Thanks to the work of neuroscientists in the 1950s who operated on cadavers and on people with brain injuries, we were able to gain a basic appreciation of the inner workings of the brain. But it wasn't until the invention of MRI, fMRI and SPECT scans in the late 2000s that neuroscience made the important breakthroughs in understanding human nature that we have today.

## THE PRE-FRONTAL CORTEX OR PROFESSOR

The professor is responsible for much of our higher-order thinking and processes. It is further subdivided into four other areas.

The dorsal professor has a strong involvement in the following core aspects of cognition:

- Working memory maintenance
- Attention
- Set-shifting (updating a behaviour when the rules change)
- Reward evaluation
- Motor planning

Next we have the dorsolateral professor, which is involved in short-term memory and impulse self-control.

The ventral professor has a function in terms of managing emotion.

The ventromedial professor helps us to be more social and to evaluate our decisions with a more long-term view rather than just for short-term gains. Let me give you a more concrete example of the role of the professor.

## THE CURIOUS CASE OF PHINEAS GAGE

In September 1843, a railroad worker called Phineas Gage sustained a horrific injury while working in Vermont. An iron bar shot up through his skull as a result of the process of rock blasting. Miraculously, he survived the accident but in the weeks and months that followed his family noticed severe changes in his personality. He changed from being a happy-go-lucky optimistic person to a sometimes volatile, moody character. His family wondered where the man they knew and loved had disappeared to.

It was believed at the time that the change in personality that resulted from his accident proved that specific aspects of personality were localised in specific areas of the brain. While a somewhat simplistic notion, in fact the current evidence we have about the brain leads us to believe that damage in very small parts of our brain can have lasting impacts on our social functioning, our working memory or even our ability to recognise other people's faces, including our partners'.

What we also know is that damage to the professor area of the brain affects someone's personality, can make them short-tempered, unsociable, quick to anger, slow to think logically and prone to impulsiveness. How many people have you met whom you believed were just being difficult, but were actually victims of mild forms of brain damage that had gone undetected? My guess is quite a few.

Stress can have a huge impact on your professor, changing the shape of this brain region. Stress in childhood may have affected how you learned to handle impulsivity and emotions. As an adult, stress can affect how you manage your attention or even how you move attention from one task to another.

In work, you may be under pressure to perform to such a high standard that small trivial tasks seem insurmountable. The need to be 'on' to such an extent, hide your emotions, and always think rationally may ultimately cause you to burn out and have an unexpected blow-up or meltdown when you least want it. Those of us who can manage our emotions effectively tend to do better than those who can't.

Suzy and Mark had a 2-year-old baby; they came to me for therapy for about six months. Mark drank too much but Suzy for her part was relentless in her criticism of Mark, it was a case of nothing he could do was ever good enough.

When he spent time with their son Thomas, it was never enough time. When he cleaned the house, she complained he needed to do it more often. During our sessions I would find myself having an emotional reaction to the way Suzy put Mark down. After about five months of therapy, and numerous attempts to help this couple understand the patterns of behaviour that were limiting their love for one another, I had to concede that this case was beyond me. Mark would shut down in the session when Suzy would rant at him. Suzy was so emotional that my logical interventions didn't seem to have any impact at all.

I suspected that Suzy had temporal lobe damage from the childhood sexual abuse she reported. Temporal lobe damage can make people have outbursts of rage, terrifying thoughts that are both dark and evil, and cause serious emotional issues. Logic goes out the window if someone has damage to the temporal lobes.

Mark went to the pub at night to escape Suzy's constant criticisms. From a brain-wise perspective, his professor had shut down and he was using alcohol to ease the stress and tension he felt from being at home. Alcohol suppresses the excitatory neurotransmitter glutamate, and it increases the inhibitory neurotransmitter

GABA. GABA or gamma-aminobutryic acid is often used as a supplement to treat anxiety.

Suzy's gorilla was over-sensitive to Mark's behaviour and body language. This was the result of earlier domestic abuse between her and Mark. His sheer mass and size was intimidating, even to me as a fit, capable male, so I could only imagine how she perceived him. Also being a male, he was a threat to Suzy at an unconscious level, a threat she responded to with attacks designed to push him away, both physically and emotionally.

The hardest part for me was to know that these screaming arguments took place while Suzy held their innocent son in her arms. Unwittingly they were causing untold stress to this helpless baby's brain.

According to Sue Gerhardt, the psychoanalytic psychotherapist, people with damage to the orbitofrontal area (OFC) of the professor 'can't relate to others sensitively. They become oblivious to social and emotional clues – they can even be sociopathic' (Gerhardt, p. 36). When we want to scream or rage at someone, the OFC acts like the control centre, monitoring to see if we are in the appropriate environment for such behaviour. What we would not do in public, we may well feel we can do at home. The OFC dictates what emotions we give expression to.

The ability to be compassionate towards others and to infer what they are feeling or thinking (Theory of Mind) depends largely on having a healthy OFC. When we are feeling rejection or shame, it is the OFC that mediates this experience for us and reduces the stress these states may cause us. This part of the brain does not mature until we are at least two years old and continues to grow throughout our childhood.

## HARRY'S MONKEYS

Harry Harlow was a psychologist working in the University of Wisconsin in the 1950s. Through experiments with rhesus monkeys, he was able to identify the importance of family relationships for how the monkeys would develop. By keeping them isolated from other monkeys, he effectively induced a state of autism in the monkeys. In humans we know that if babies are deprived of human contact during the first three years of their lives, they may lose their abilities to relate properly to others.

A second experiment he performed involved allowing a baby monkey to choose from two types of surrogate mothers. One was a wire-framed monkey that could feed the baby monkey milk. The other was a cloth monkey that had no food to offer. Which surrogate do you think the monkey chose? He ran to the cloth monkey every time. In fact, the baby monkey stayed cuddling the cloth monkey for 18 hours despite receiving no food.

In humans the amount of loving touch we receive shapes the development of our brain, and specifically the professor, predisposing us to make connections with the people around us. Each brain is plastic or malleable so it's shaped differently depending on the adults and environment in question. This allows us to adapt successfully to those around us and ensures that we're fully equipped to get our needs met.

So how could you recognise if you or your partner is dealing with a low-functioning professor? Here's a handy checklist:

- Are you feeling lazy or disinterested in activities?
- Are you noticing a lack of inspiration in your life?
- Are you easily distracted and lacking focus?
- Are you feeling overly emotional or lacking clarity about your role?

As a consequence of feeling this way, we may start to nitpick on our partners' faults, we may blame them for our own sense of dissatisfaction with life, and we may even seek novel ideas to cheer ourselves up (even if those ideas are unaffordable or unrealistic such as moving house or going on an expensive holiday). Nagging has its roots in a faulty professor.

A general feeling of restlessness can creep over us and we can start to overindulge in food or drink, stop exercising and become extremely lethargic. How many arguments have *you* caused in your relationship because your professor wasn't functioning correctly?

The solution is to make space away from work, away from smartphones, away from the house. Get out into nature as much as possible, even if it's raining. Put on your rain gear and let your five senses come alive with the sights, smells, sounds and experiences of the world around you. It's time to ground yourself and to breathe deeply so that you can once more experience a balance in this 'executive' area of the brain. Once you do this, your relationship with yourself, your family and your spouse will regain the balance it has lost.

## THE BASAL GANGLIA OR TOOTHBRUSH

What part of the brain do you think is responsible for our habits or, more importantly, our addictions?

Thanks to new research we can now pin-point more accurately where these aspects of our behaviour are located. The toothbrush is a group of cells, billions of them, in fact, that control our ability to form and maintain routines and habits.

The website neuroscientificallychallenged.com has the following useful description of the role of the basal ganglia.

> The toothbrush receives information about a desired goal from the cerebral cortex; they help to achieve that goal by selecting the appropriate action for it and initiating movement while at the same time ensuring that oppositional movements are inhibited. The result is smooth, fluid movement. We can see the importance of the toothbrush in movement by looking at the overt symptoms of someone with Parkinson's disease. These symptoms involve slow movement, tremors, and rigidity, and their severity is associated with the neurodegeneration of toothbrush nuclei and their connecting pathways.

If your husband comes home from work, sits down on the sofa, opens the newspaper, switches on the TV, kicks off his shoes and totally tunes out to your demands for help with the kids, feel free to curse his toothbrush. The neurotransmitter dopamine plays a key role in the toothbrush. A neurotransmitter is a chemical that communicates a signal across a synapse. A synapse is the gap between two neurons. Dopamine controls reward-seeking behaviour and so, when we search out thrills from sex, or take enjoyment from fast food or chocolate, dopamine floods our brains.

The problem with habits is that they are unconscious: we don't think about them, we just do them. For many of us the habit of nagging happens so often that we don't even realise we are doing it. So when our partner tunes out to our requests for them to change, we may have no idea how vociferous we were or how demanding we sounded.

To improve our relationships, we need to become aware of our daily routines, from how we may leave dirty dishes around the kitchen to tuning out our partners' conversations. We need to start getting those billions of ganglia to work in our favour and not against us. By doing this we can stop being on autopilot and more critically analyse what it is we do that might be causing our relationship to suffer.

## THE STRIATUM OR REWARD CENTRE

The reward centre is located deep inside the basal ganglia and plays a crucial role in reward, motivation and addiction. We get a surge of dopamine in the nucleus accumbens, part of the reward centre, when we think we are going to receive a gift of money or when hetrosexual men see pictures of beautiful women. When events are novel or unusual we tend to remember them better than routine ones: this functionality is also located in the reward centre.

So what does this mean for your relationship? Put simply, the rewards you give or receive in your relationship play a role in what you remember as important in the relationship. In other words, we often only focus on the memory of the bad things that happened to us and not the good things. This then deactivates our reward centre and makes us less likely to do other nice things for our partners. A vicious cycle ensues and marital satisfaction drops off rapidly. Negative routines are therefore your biggest enemy. To rekindle love once more, you need to do nice things often enough for your partner's brain to be rewired towards this expectancy.

When we know what is important to our partner in how they define love, then we have some chance of letting them feel special. Some people like to *hear* the words 'I love you', others need love to be *demonstrated* in the form of material possessions, and for other people holding hands is all they need to feel loved and secure. Usually, how we want love to be expressed to us comes from our childhoods. If your parents were poor when you were growing up, you might need a partner to demonstrate their love for you through expensive gifts in an unconscious attempt to rectify the poverty you experienced as a child. Each of us is different and unique, that's the beauty of it, and the challenge.

## THE INSULAR CORTEX OR FULL-LENGTH MIRROR

In Anthony de Mello's seminal book, *Awareness*, he likened awareness to waking up and being able to see all around you. What de Mello didn't discuss because, in fairness to him, no one knew, was where exactly in the brain we can locate personal awareness. Now we think we know. It's in a brain part called the insular cortex or 'full-length mirror'.

The full-length mirror is responsible for regulating our emotions, perception and interpersonal experience. While I might be giving the impression that each separate area of the brain is responsible for distinct and separate functions, the reality is a little more complicated. Remember that there are billions of neurons in our brains, all interconnected to one another in a multitude of ways, all sending vast amounts of electrical signals, with different instructions to each area.

For the sake of brevity we can talk about certain sections of the brain having certain functions, but it would be more accurate to say that many of the brain areas work interdependently with one another. A car engine has many parts, but not every engine part is linked to every other part. It's easy to state the specific functions of the oil filter or spark plug: not so with the brain.

Antonio Damasio, the Portuguese neuroscientist, postulated that the full-length mirror plays a big role in what he calls the 'somatic marker hypothesis'. This is the belief that rational thinking can't be separated from feelings. Many of us believe that we have feelings of happiness, sadness, fear or anger and that we equally have separate thoughts of happiness, sadness, fear and anger. What Damasio proposes is that each of us has a unique way of experiencing the chemical reactions in our bodies, including hormones, that we filter these experiences to match our world view, and then afterwards we have thoughts about these reactions, which, for us, confirm the validity of what we are experiencing. In other words, our feelings influence our thoughts and vice versa – more than we know.

## WHEN TWO BRAINS GO TO A WEDDING

Jane is getting ready to attend a wedding of a good friend of Steve's. She puts on her make-up and her dress, spending ages making sure that she looks fabulous. Steve was ready about an hour before Jane so he has been playing with the children and keeping them entertained. Playtime is getting a little difficult and the kids are starting to act out somewhat and Steve is finding it quite tough going. Frustrated that Jane still isn't ready, he shouts upstairs, 'Are you nearly ready, Jane?' She replies, 'Nearly.'

Just then one of the glass bowls that the children were playing with smashes on the floor, shattering glass everywhere. In a panic to clean up before a minor accident occurs, Steve fails to hear Jane appear at the bottom of the stairs and ask, 'So how do I look?' Annoyed that he has ignored her, she repeats much more loudly, 'Well, how do I look then?' He snaps at her in frustration, 'You look bloody fabulous as always; now, are you going to help me here or not?'

When they arrive at the reception, Jane and Steve are seated between two other couples. On Jane's side is a quiet, shy couple, on Steve's side is a loud, funny and engaging couple. As the meal goes on, and Jane's attempts to maintain a conversation are snubbed by her 'table-mates' while Steve and his new-found friends are having a rip-roaring time, Jane sinks further and further into a slump. Eventually, she leaves the table and returns ten minutes later with her eyeliner and mascara smeared. She had been crying in the bathroom.

So what happened in their brains for them to experience the same event so differently?

Well, back in the bedroom, as she looked in the mirror, Jane remembered at an unconscious level how often her parents would mock her previous attempts to look nice: 'Sure who's going to be looking at you?' they would sneer. This caused a flood of adrenaline and cortisol to shoot through her brain. The full-length mirror became aware of this surge of electrical activity and tried to make sense of it. Jane also noticed an empty sensation in her tummy, which she dismissed as hunger, but also a vague sense of emptiness in her chest area, which she couldn't quite understand.

Upon finishing her preparation, she hoped that Steve would validate her by praising her and indicating how attractive he found her. Her reward systems lit up in anticipation of this approval and had Steve cooperated properly her cortisol and adrenaline levels would have gone back to normal. But the opposite happened and an argument ensued, leading her to feel even more physically unsettled inside. The icing on the cake was the way the shy couple ignored her at the wedding.

Had Jane come from a loving family she would have approved of herself rather than expecting Steve to. During the 'big reveal', after noticing the smashed glass, she would have offered Steve her full support rather than demanding praise. At the dinner table at the wedding, she would have extricated herself from Mr and Mrs Boring, and sat beside Steve and his new-found friends.

I propose that you take a minute every day to answer the following questions:

- How do I feel now?
- What feelings did I have today?
- Did I experience the world as a positive place or as a dangerous place?
- What might I do differently tomorrow to increase the happiness I could feel?
- What do I want from tonight?
- Do I need support, comfort, attention or none of the above?
- How do I imagine my partner is feeling?
- What does she/he need from me?
- If I have children, how will they react when they see me?
- What do they need from me?

In doing this you will become more skilled at slowing down your reactions to everyday stresses and bring more rational responses into play, rather than emotionally fuelled ones.

The majority of us never take stock before we get home. I did a private marriage course a number of years back and the couple had a 6-month-old baby in the kitchen while we were working. The man admitted that he was stressed out of his mind. He was handed the baby every day as soon as he came home from work, while he still had his coat on; that's how immediate the changeover was. I advised him to wait outside in the car before coming in for about five minutes, just to calm down and ground himself. The worst thing we can do as parents is bring our work stress home with us and then handle a small baby. The baby will sense our stress and become stressed itself.

## THE AMYGDALA OR GORILLA

Deep within our brain structure is a small almond-shaped cluster of neurons called the amygdala. It has two sides: the left and the right. Each side has certain functions in relation to the regulation of emotion. The 'gorilla' manages our emotional responses to the environment but it gives preference to registering fear over anything else. This is an ancient survival tool that evolved deep within our brains to keep us safe and recognise threats.

It's believed that the gorilla plays a role in depression, anxiety, post-traumatic stress disorder and how much pleasure we are allowed to derive from our environment.

So with our fictional couple, for example, Jane is always full of fear and anxiety when she meets Steve as he comes home from work. What she doesn't realise is that her gorilla is over-active, seeking out reasons to justify this fear and that any action Steve makes that can be interpreted as negative will lead Jane to feel abandoned, unloved or unappreciated. Steve hasn't a chance.

## THE ANTERIOR CINGULATE CORTEX OR INNER SHERLOCK

You know how I said earlier that the brain is a very complex organ and that we can't just neatly pick a brain area and describe exactly what that area does? We take this fact to a whole new level when we try to understand the insular cortex. Over the last 50 years, researchers have argued about the function of this brain region. For the sake of brevity and your sanity, I am going to keep this section as simple as possible.

We now know, thanks to groundbreaking work by Srinivasan S. Pillay, that emotional support and positive social interactions can quieten that part of our brain called the anterior cingulate cortex (ACC), which then relieves distress. However, when we focus all our attention on where our pain lies, either emotional or physical, the brain registers this as more painful than it really is. What we pay attention to grows, in other words. If we only think about what is wrong with our relationship and not what is working well, we will feel uneasy all the time. This feeling comes from the activation of the inner Sherlock.

In Jane's case, her focus was on her own insecurity from the time she saw her reflection in the mirror to the time she perceived she was being excluded from the wedding fun. This was magnified more and more with each experience she had as her ACC continued to focus on all that it perceived was wrong, rather than stopping to check if she was possibly overreacting.

Whenever there is conflict, there is ACC activation. This means that every time you argue with your partner, both ACCs are active. 'When it detects conflict, it tells the rest of the brain to act in accordance with this,' explains Pillay (Pillay, p. 198). The ACC scans your environment and brings your attention to relevant areas such as your partner's body language, tone of voice and seating position. It's able to send messages from your unconscious to your conscious. In other words, if your partner calls you a lazy so and so and that happens to be exactly what your father called you, the ACC will recall that fact and make you hyper-aware of the anger you felt years ago. This will make the current argument even more difficult to resolve.

The majority of couples who seek my help are doing so because their unconscious brains are remembering childhood emotional pain that they now believe is being caused by their partner. In reality, if they had had better childhoods, their partner's behaviour would not affect them nearly as much.

Pillay has devised an ingenious way to tame the inner Sherlock. He suggests using the following actions: resolve, reassess, refocus, re-engage and reframe.

- **Resolve:** Look at the source of the conflict and try to resolve it before doing anything else.
- **Reassess:** Is your perception all that accurate?
- **Re-engage:** With each other through meaningful dialogue.
- **Refocus:** Turn your attention to the benefits of their visit.
- **Reframe:** Take a different perspective on the same problem and see what it looks like.

## The Hypothalamus or Thermostat

One of the most important functions of the 'thermostat' is to link the nervous system to the pituitary glands via the endocrine system. This brain region regulates our temperature, our sexual behaviour and impulses, our intake of food and water, and mediates our emotional responses to situations around us.

The thermostat releases vasopressin and oxytocin, two chemicals involved in love and bonding.

## The Hippocampus or USB Stick

This brain area is responsible for long-term memory. If we experience distress in our marriage, the 'USB stick' may activate. Why would it do this? It could be because our partners may do or say something that reminds us of an earlier painful childhood experience. In fact, some would argue that the reason people tolerate abusive relationships is because as children they were physically beaten by their parents or guardians, and the USB stick draws upon this memory, i.e. a memory of helplessness that overrides the functioning of their professor, which is screaming 'Get out now.'

## The Brain as a Hand

If you have made it this far I commend you. Well done. After all this technical information, I would like to share with you a reductionist way of conceptualising the brain. If you search for 'the brain hand model' on YouTube, you will be rewarded with a video of Dr Dan Siegel, the Californian therapist and brain expert, demonstrating how the brain can be understood, using his hand.

## Do Men and Women Have Different Brains?

Yes, but not as much as you might think. Women have thicker connections between the left and right sides of their brains so they can process language earlier and better than men. The corpus callosum, which connects the two hemispheres of the brain, is 30 per cent thicker in women than in men, according to Martha Bridge Denckla, a research scientist at Kennedy Krieger Institute.

David Geary, professor of psychological sciences at the University of Missouri, argues that women retain a greater ability to manipulate language than men, and this probably had an evolutionary function in allowing women to gain some advantages over their stronger male counterparts. He believes that 'the frontal area of the cortex and the temporal area of the cortex are more precisely organized in women, and are bigger in volume' (http://www.webmd.com/balance/features/how-male-female-brains-differ?page=2).

In practice, these differences mean that men say less than women, form connections through presence rather than conversation, and prefer to work out their problems by themselves rather than sharing the problem with their partners.

Once we recognise that this is who we are, and that's okay, we can save ourselves pointless stress. Too many couples argue over the consequences of their brain differences. Why bother? We can't change them.

# 8

## PARENTING YOUR BRAIN

Has Anyone Seen My Libido?

A Day in the Life

Can Brain Science Make You a
Better Parent?

## DR DANIEL AMEN

At 3 o'clock on a Saturday afternoon, Larry Kavorski sat in the busy waiting room of one of the world's leading brain doctors, Daniel Amen. He was there for a SPECT scan, a tool that Dr Amen uses to take photographs of the human brain. Larry was the father of two children, one 3 years old and the other 13 months. Larry had been feeling fatigued lately, and his doctor had referred him to Dr Amen. If you have never seen one, a SPECT scanner looks similar to an MRI machine; you lie prostrate underneath the scanner as it scans your brain. Thirty minutes later, it was time for the analysis.

Larry discovered that his brain was no longer healthy. Dr Amen showed him the coloured areas on his chart and what they signified. Larry had the brain of a 50-year-old man though he was just 35. What had caused this rapid deterioration in his brain tissue?

Like many, Larry had adopted some bad brain habits since becoming a parent. His exercise regime was almost non-existent. He drank a bottle of wine mid-week, and then two more at the weekend. Having previously watched his diet and ensured a good mix of fruit and vegetables, he was now surviving on processed food and as much sugar as he could handle. Larry was severely stressed. Being alone all day with two small children meant that Larry was experiencing withdrawal symptoms from human contact. With no one to speak to, or to get support from, he was at severe risk of developing full-blown depression.

At night, Larry drank coffee as a reward for having survived a hectic day. Caffeine blocks adenosine, a chemical that tells us to sleep. He also checked Facebook and other social-media websites on his smartphone while lying in bed. This kept him awake, inhibited melatonin being released into his brain (melatonin is a hormone that regulates other hormones and manages the body's sleep cycle), and the lack of sleep subsequently caused him to lose motivation for exercise.

Having gained weight, Larry no longer wanted his partner Damien to touch him in a sexual way, so as a couple they both suffered from the absence of oxytocin and vasopressin. Not feeling the bonding effects of the love chemicals meant they were growing further and further apart. Is Larry's situation unusual? Not at all: in fact, it's the norm.

Thanks to the work of Dr Amen, we can now say that the fallout from parenting (rather than parenting itself) can severely damage your brain, causing premature aging and brain-tissue deterioration. For some mothers and fathers, 'baby brain' is real as the brain sheds neural connections that it no longer deems useful; if you're not using them, you won't retain them.

Cognitive functioning can be reduced by lack of usage, which, for some parents, undermines their confidence in rejoining the workforce. Many women (and some men) have given up careers not because they wanted to, but because in the five or so years of being out of the workforce their ability to think critically, to analyse rationally and to reason deductively may have suffered while caring full-time for children. An entirely different set of skills may indeed have been learned, but this may not provide sufficient reassurance that rejoining the workforce would be a success.

When couples come to my office for therapy, one of the first areas I explore is around children, do they have any and if so how many? Tanya and Clive had two children when they came to see me last year, so I began the session as follows: 'So, you have two children? Ah okay, if I'm not mistaken they're probably depriving you both of sleep, relaxation, money and sex.' They nodded in agreement. 'So knowing all this, how can I help you both?'

At this point every couple, including Tanya and Clive, look at each other and laugh. It's like finally someone acknowledges that their lives are stressful and it's not their fault.

I was chatting with one of my friends' husbands recently, a proud dad of two 4-year-old boys. 'How has it been?' I asked.

'Hell,' he replied.

The majority of couples with children can expect the following issues to arise: lack of sleep, lack of sex, lack of romance, lack of personal space, lack of time for the couple, lack of money, lack of personal resources, lack of physical affection, etc. There is no question in my mind but that the majority of brains of the parents I work with are in some form of distress. So from a brain-science perspective, what is happening?

Let's start with sleep. Sleep plays an important role in memory formation and in our ability to learn new tasks. Not sleeping at night and having to care for a baby is extremely challenging. Driving to work having been awake at 4 a.m. and 6 a.m., changed three or four nappies, struggled through a few bottle feeds while at the same time trying to motivate yourself to give a presentation is just not good for you. Melatonin is the chemical in our brains that causes sleep. It's activated by darkness, and light impedes its production. So checking Facebook or reading on your smartphone late at night will prevent you sleeping. The blue-light photons emitted from smartphones also prevent melatonin release.

The absence of sleep makes most people impatient and intolerant, two traits that are not that useful for maintaining a healthy relationship. As a result of sleep deprivation, even the most trivial of issues can become a raging storm of fury and discontent. Some couples then resort to bickering and scorekeeping. These are more of the behaviours that chip away at the store of goodwill you feel for someone.

Marriage expert John Gottman calls the amount of goodwill couples feel for one another the 'Love Bank'. Without frequent deposits in our love banks, such as offers of support or affection, couples can literally run out of love for each other.

One of the initial stressors facing parents is the sheer volume and intensity of the infant's cries. In 2007, Kerstein Sander of the Leibniz Institute for Neurobiology measured the intensity of a baby's cries. She played a series of recordings of a baby's cries to a number of volunteers, and observed a significant reaction in their amygdala and anterior cingulate cortices, more so in the women's than in the men's. She felt that this proved women had a genetic disposition to be more attentive to a baby's cries than men. At one point when my daughter was just three weeks old, she had serious pain that we couldn't quite locate. We took her to hospital. Two nurses, three consultants and three loving adults, i.e. her parents and grandmother, all stood around a hospital bed as this little creature, only one foot tall, screamed in agony as we slowly found out where the pain was located. It moved her family to tears. That's what her cries were designed to do.

I remember reading that governments have been using sleep deprivation in detention centres located in secret bases around the world, forcing prisoners to listen to loud, wailing noises just as they were about to fall asleep. This is done repeatedly to prisoners as a very cruel form of torture.

## HAS ANYONE SEEN MY LIBIDO?

The lack of sex for couples with children has taken on mythological proportions, and has been the stuff of stand-up comedy for years. I genuinely believed this was just an urban legend, that there was no way one's sex drive could fall off so rapidly, or that it would be that hard to motivate oneself to have sex. I was wrong. Once you overcome the tiredness of parenting, there is the fear that sex may lead to another pregnancy, and unless this is something that you want, it can become a psychological hurdle.

'Without romance there can be no desire,' I'm often heard telling couples at my marriage courses. On reflection, I honestly can't remember the last time I bought my partner flowers, or did anything romantic. (Note to self: buy flowers.) When every day is a struggle to survive, romance will take a back seat. As couples, we need to feel rewarded for the efforts we put into our relationships. We need and crave dopamine, adrenaline and epinephrine, all the 'love chemicals' we felt when we entered those heady days and nights of our early romances. When we stop having sex with our partners due to lack of libido or exhaustion, we miss the positive impact on our relationship that is derived from oxytocin and vasopressin.

For both men and women, sex and affection are crucial components of love. Bitterness and resentment can often be the by-product of a lack of sex in a relationship. This is the very opposite of what the endogenous opioids, the range of chemicals in our brain that impact positively on our overall mood, are designed to make us feel. Many couples feel cheated by life at this point. Brains are flooded with cortisol. Stress and conflict dominate their exchanges where once there was only affection and connection.

Edel was 47 years old when she came to see me. Her husband Mike worked hard at a nearby factory. He put in long hours to provide a good quality of life for his wife and four children. They came for therapy because Edel felt that she was missing something from her life. A number of sessions with the couple together were not really helping, so I asked her to come in by herself.

At this point, Edel admitted that her employer, a wealthy plastic surgeon, was in love with her, and she with him. She couldn't help but imagine what life would be like without the chaos of the breakfast routines, shuffling the kids out to the childminder, racing to the shops to buy dinner, cleaning the house, falling on to the couch too exhausted even to watch TV. Weekends were worse, she said; no childminder.

At work, Edel was experiencing the dopamine rushes we mentioned earlier. Each sexy smile she and her boss shared released a chemical cascade in her brain that helped her suspend reality and imagine a better life. In fact, most affairs, in my opinion, start this way, through boredom with routines and the need to escape reality. If the affair is revealed, however, the consequences can be devastating. Heartbreak is real: it's the withdrawal of opioids from the brain, leading to a profound feeling of loss and emptiness.

## A Day in the Life

It might be a good idea to plot what happens in the brain of a parent on a typical day just to give us a clearer picture of how it can be so stressful.

Jane takes her two children shopping to the local shopping centre. Aged five and three, both children are at a difficult age. When they get to the shopping centre, her eldest, Nathan, runs away from Jane towards his favourite toy shop, leaving Jane and Chrissie far behind. Chrissie kicks off at this point as she wants to run too but is being held back by Jane. On the way to retrieve Nathan, mother and daughter pass a confectionary shop with a large plastic ice-cream cone outside. Chrissie stops and refuses to walk any further until Jane buys her a cone. Jane refuses. Chrissie then hurls herself on the floor and starts screaming at full pitch. Jane verbally reprimands her to no avail. Just then Nathan comes back holding a Star Wars figure he took (accidentally) from the toy shop. Three or four onlookers gather at this point and start muttering and glancing over at Jane. Two stressful hours later, Jane gets the children home in one piece, where she meets Steve who had been playing golf that day. So what happens next?

Steve walks into the kitchen where both children are quietly eating their tea. Jane is preparing the adults' dinner.

Steve: Well kids, how are you doing? Did you have a great day shopping with Mum?
Both kids smile and nod.
Steve: Ah that's great, and did you behave yourselves for Mum?
Both nod once more.

Relieved, Steve approaches Jane from behind and nuzzles into her neck. Jane, tears of frustration in her eyes, swivels around holding the bread knife, almost catching Steve's shirt. She apologises then runs out of the kitchen and up the stairs, leaving Steve wondering what's just happened.

Throughout the day Jane's feelings could be summed up as follows: overwhelmed, fear, anxiety, anger, resentment, exhaustion, despair, sadness, relief and frustration. Steve's feelings could be summed up with one word: contentment.

Playing golf gave him the benefit of thinking time, alone time, social time, competition time and reconnection time. This was somewhat different than his wife's experience. Jane's time with her children had activated the following brain parts:

- Her gorilla
- Her full-length mirror
- Her inner Sherlock
- Her toothbrush
- Her professor
- Her thermostat
- Her USB stick

A brain-science description of this incident may look something like this: the gorilla, which processes emotions, gave priority to Jane's fear when she saw Nathan running away from her. The full-length mirror, which processes her internal life, was activated when Jane started to compare herself with single, attractive, childless women at the shopping centre. Her mind raced with questions such as, 'Is this what I can look forward to for the rest of my life?' Not feeling attractive caused her to doubt herself and to question her life choices. Jane's inner Sherlock, which detects conflict, lit up when she realised how nice the kids were being to Steve and the lies they were telling him. Realising this, Jane became enraged that there was an issue here that was going unnoticed.

The toothbrush area of Jane's brain, which controls her habits and routines, helped Jane to stay on autopilot throughout the day. This meant that she was disconnected from her emotions when it might have been more useful to stop and tune into them.

The thermostat, which is active in controlling her glands, was releasing chemicals to manage Jane's survival needs. Unfortunately, due to the chaos of her day, Jane did not eat well or drink enough fluids, so her body suffered, too, not just her brain. The brain, like all our organs, needs nourishment.

Finally, while Jane was trying to cope with Chrissie's tantrum, her USB stick had released memories of Jane's childhood when her mother had successfully taken all four children on shopping trips and always did so while remaining calm and in control.

These memories percolated at an unconscious level and left Jane with a gnawing feeling that she wasn't a good enough mother. Jane also noticed the bystanders judging her competency as a mother, enflaming her inner Sherlock, which monitors for fairness. This left her feeling resentful of her local community, which, rather than help her, preferred to stand and judge.

From a practical point of view, what could Steve have done differently if he had access to this information?

For a start, he could have had more contact with Jane throughout the day. He could have encouraged Jane to make sure that she had some form of support while he wasn't available.

When he came home, perhaps he might first have spoken to Jane and not to the kids. Ideally, he should have called her before arriving home to ask if she needed him to reprimand the children. If he had allowed her to frame the day as she had experienced it, it would have validated her and allowed her time to defuse some of her anger.

Awareness of our partners' stresses is a key component in creating bonds between us. Is it any wonder that so many relationships fall apart if childrearing is mismanaged? Separations and divorces due to conflicts over parenting are more common than we want to acknowledge. A consequence of divorce for large numbers of men and women is depression. Left untreated, depression can lead to suicidal ideation and even suicide itself. So to get back to my original question, can parenting cause brain damage? Not really, but the stress from parenting can.

Perhaps it's a bit extreme but is there some merit in what that sage, Homer Simpson, said, that 'Marriage is like a coffin, and each kid is another nail'? Of course not, children are wonderful.

## CAN BRAIN SCIENCE MAKE YOU A BETTER PARENT?

I will never forget this family. In front of me sat the parents, a daughter (17), 4-year-old Lucy, and a grandmother. The family needed help because Dad's temper was out of control. Angry at his financial circumstances and lack of employment, Dad was like a grenade waiting to explode. His mother-in-law lived with them and given how small the house was, this added even more pressure to this overstretched family. Mum and Dad were struggling to cope with the fact that their older daughter had announced a few months previously that she was gay. Being Catholic, they found this hard to come to terms with. My focus, however, was on Lucy.

Bright-blonde hair and piercing blue eyes, Lucy sat quietly on a cushion in front of her parents. I was mesmerised by her facial expressions. She seemed wise beyond her years. I started the session by asking her what she hoped to get from chatting with everyone in the room.

Lucy spoke at length about how Mammy and Daddy are angry all the time with her sister and how 'Nanny tries to stop them shouting at each other but they don't listen to Nanny, either.' I asked Lucy how she felt when Mammy and Daddy shouted at each other. 'I feel hot inside,' she said. Her parents were stunned. They had no idea that their arguments were hurting Lucy.

As the session progressed, we explored what everyone could do differently to help Lucy feel better. It was a very moving experience and it seemed that this 4-year-old had the power to heal the family's wounds. Dad cried and put Lucy on his lap, promising never to shout again. Mum held Lucy's hands and kissed them. Lucy's sister told Lucy that from now on she was going to take her more often to the local playground, so she could feel like a little girl again. Lucy's grandmother told Lucy that she was the most important little girl in the world and she was to always tell Nanny if she was upset. The memory of this session even now brings tears to my eyes.

Lucy's feeling of being 'hot inside' was most likely the result of cortisol, the stress chemical, coursing through her brain.

Being so young meant she was unable to calm herself down and needed the loving embrace of a family member to do so. It was great to see Dad cuddle her. Thanks to neural plasticity, this family could help each other rewire each other's brains. Over the next three sessions, I explained to the adults in the family the importance of affection for Lucy and of creating a peaceful and stress-free home. Thankfully, everyone came on board and all was well again at our six-month review stage.

In *The Neuroscience of Human Relationships*, Louis Cozolino posits the idea that the human brain develops best when it's interconnected with other human beings. Think of the Romanian orphans during Ceauşescu's regime, left untouched in cribs for months or years. Their social brains were seriously damaged by the isolation they experienced.

Let me give you an example from my own life about the fragility of our earliest experiences of being social beings. Just today while I was driving with my daughter in the back of the car, I telephoned her mother at work to complain that I was unable to work on this book as our childminder was unwell and I needed support. My partner was on loudspeaker for the entire conversation and, when I hung up, I turned around to check on my daughter. She was looking forlornly out the rear window. I called her five times but, most unusually, she wouldn't even look at me. I finally realised what had happened. Éabha had heard Breige chatting to me but Mum had completely ignored Éabha, which is why she looked so sad.

I rang Breige back immediately and put her on to Éabha. At this point Éabha perked up and started giggling. She is just 18 months old and her brain had registered that this was a time when Mum didn't care enough to speak with her. In just 60 seconds she had felt unloved and unwanted and her facial expressions told me of her upset. Luckily, I was attuned to her emotionally and was able to rectify the problem immediately.

The experience of this social rejection would have triggered her insular cortex and her anterior cingulate cortex, i.e. the full-length mirror and inner Sherlock. Continuous feelings of rejection on a daily basis have a detrimental impact on a child's brain. Children tend to shut down emotionally. Parents sometimes mistake this for moodiness rather than rejection.

If we were to adopt a neuroscientific approach to raising children, what would we do differently? And if we used brain-science principles to raise our children, would this improve our own relationships, too?

Contrary to popular opinion, a baby's brain is not fully developed when it's born. It undergoes rapid growth and development for the first two years. Your baby's brain is very vulnerable to external influences or stresses. You as a parent probably don't realise how powerful your touch, your voice or even your smile is in shaping your baby's brain. A process called 'pruning' is undertaken in the infant's brain, which means that neurons that are not used are shed by the brain. In fact, 90 per cent of the growth of the human brain happens in the first five years of life. Many of these neural connections grow in response to your relationship with your baby. At about seven years of age, this process slows down and the connections become more stable, meaning more of your child's personality has been hard-wired by this point.

At birth, each child has a number of internal systems that help them to deal with life. These are the rage system, the fear system and the separation distress system. These help the child to cope with the challenges that early life presents. These systems release chemicals in your child's brain that may help or hinder the brain's growth.

Cozolino states that 'our parents are the primary environment to which our young brains adapt, and their unconscious minds are our first reality' (Cozolino, p. 7). Some clients in therapy are there because they had negative experiences in the first three years of their lives. The problem for most people is that memory had not developed at that point, so clients have no conscious awareness of those events. All they have are their current symptoms, to highlight that they don't feel as content as they think they should.

## CAN YOU SPOIL A CHILD WITH LOVE?

Whenever I take my family to see the grandparents, and they see me being effusive with my child, they often comment to me that the child is spoiled. She receives no sugar or treats, never watches TV and is never bought toys unless there is a need for novelty or stimulation. What they are referring to is the amount of affection, attention and adoration that she is shown. Could too much affection be bad for children?

Not according to groundbreaking work done by Jay Belsky in London. Professor Belsky has been studying the impact of parenting effectiveness for many years now. In his research, Belsky notes that physical affection is crucial to the development of a child's brain. Being touched by Mum and Dad at the appropriate times and in the appropriate ways gives the baby's brain the ability to regulate itself and allows the child to feel more secure in the world. Contrast this with how babies who are handled roughly by parents will come to experience the world. In later life, they may believe that the world is a scary place, that people should not be trusted and that being anxious is normal.

A common mistake parents make is believing that being affectionate with their children may inhibit resilience in the child. While it's true that some stress can be helpful to a child's growth, it's more important that they are held lovingly, supported through their scariest feelings, and are allowed the opportunity to reach out for affection and to know they will receive it once they do. So no, you can't spoil a child with love.

What does all this mean for couples who want better relationships? As a rule, I now make it my business to do a full baby-to-childhood background check with my clients to see if the reason they are not getting on together is related to poor brain functioning rather than present-day issues.

Separation issues in early childhood have been linked to depression and relationship issues in adults. If my clients were left in day care from an early age and had no loving adults consistently meeting their needs, their brains suffered. Dr Belsky has written extensively on the effects of bad day care on a baby's development. When you think about it, it's not rocket science. We all need to feel loved in our relationships. If our partners become cold, unsupportive or refuse to be affectionate with us, it really hurts.

So picture the scene. A baby girl, Jessie, is woken from her deep sleep each morning, dressed and put into a cold car seat, and handed a bottle by which she feeds herself. Forty minutes later, Jessie is handed to a complete stranger in the day-care centre. From this point on, how many times is Jessie smiled at, held gently, spoken to, soothed when she cries, laughed at and played with? Loving parents will do these activities without thinking. In doing so, they help to regulate what we call Jessie's parasympathetic nervous system. This system regulates her breathing, her bowel movements and her appetite. In day care, when Jessie feels alone and afraid, her gorilla becomes hypersensitive and her fragile brain tries to make sense of her feelings. Her hormones will fluctuate and just like you feel when waiting for a big interview, everything tenses up and her appetite may be affected.

As an adult, you might be able to calm yourself down before an interview. As a baby in day care, you just don't have this ability. Jessie will reach out to have her needs met and may cry more. Hopefully, she will be responded to with love. In many cases, however, this does not happen. At this point, Jessie shuts down emotionally. When her parents collect her they only see a quiet, sullen infant. They can't see her distress. When researchers have measured the cortisol levels of babies like Jessie, they have found their stress levels to be sky-high, even though there were no outward signs whatsoever.

From the time we are born to the time we die, we need to feel that people are interested in us, are fascinated by us and long to be in our company. When we place our child in a crèche or with a childminder, we need to be sure that our child will experience this same sense of belonging and warmth. If they don't, we may be setting them up to feel rejection later in life. Just yesterday, I watched a childminder completely ignore a toddler during lunch with her friends. What message does this send to a developing brain? Children need to feel they are at the centre of an adult's world, no matter who the adult is.

When we behave unkindly to a child, or if we provide care that is out of touch with the child's needs, this signals to the child that the world is not a safe place and that they should not explore it. Children who are apart from their parents for long stretches may feel unloved and abandoned by their parents, but have no way of communicating this to them. As adults, they may not know how to express their needs to their partner, or they might not expect those needs to be met, even if they can express them.

Ian and Clare, an English couple living in Ireland, were married 20 years when they came to see me. Ian complained that Clare never wanted to have sex with him. She said that she was quite happy to do what other wives did, which, in her mind, was to take life easy now that their three children had left home. Clare became quickly defensive when we explored the importance of physical affection for sustaining relationships, especially marital ones. She said that was his agenda, not hers. Why should she be expected to have sex when she didn't feel like it?

The issue of non-sexual affection was discussed, too. Again Clare was quite adamant that if she didn't want to kiss or hug Ian, why should she have to? In one of the sessions I asked Clare if she loved Ian. She said, 'Of course I love him; I just don't want to have to touch him when I don't feel like it.'

Further exploration with the couple revealed that Clare's mum had returned to work soon after she was born. She was then cared for by a grandmother who she remembered as being cold and angry most of the time.

During a one-to-one session, I wondered with Clare if her grandmother had been able to meet her emotional needs. Clare said she didn't see how that was possible, given that her grandmother was in her late sixties at the time, and also worked on the family farm. Her earliest memory was of standing in the doorway of the farmhouse, aged just four, in floods of tears because her mum wasn't there to soothe her after she fell and cut her knee. Granny just shouted at her and told her to get out of the house.

Clare had never been able to regulate her emotions properly, without the loving support of both her parents. The absence of oxytocin, serotonin, dopamine and norepinephrine in her brain as it matured affected her ability not only to receive love, but to give love, in this case in the physical form of affection or sex.

Eight months after the couple left therapy, I received a phone call from Ian. He wanted to know if having an affair would be justified given Clare's refusal to have sex. I was at a loss for words.

## THE BLUE SPOT

The locus coeruleus (meaning 'blue spot') is a structure deep in your brain stem that becomes active when something of real significance is happening. If, for example, you and your child, if you have one, or your partner if you don't have children, are experiencing a really wonderful moment of connection, something you both realise has significance for you both, at this point the locus coeruleus will spring into action and shower the brain with norepinephrine. This then cements the experience into your memory.

For children, this means that the more fun you have with them, the stronger the connection they feel with you. By the time they collect their children from day care, many parents are too exhausted to delight in anything, except getting the children to bed.

In our modern society, many of us experience stress levels that our brains just can't cope with. As bad as this is, it's exacerbated if the brain in question is only five years old. A stressed brain that is not fully developed can hold high levels of CRF (corticotrophin-releasing factor), which can in turn block the release of positive arousal chemicals like dopamine and serotonin. When this happens, the child can experience outbursts of irritation or rage. Stress also releases another chemical in the brain called acetylcholine. This chemical helps us to feel alert and to concentrate, that's the good part; the bad part is that it can also leave people angry, hostile or irritated.

Can you think back to your own childhood or ask your parents if you experienced much stress as a child? What caused the stress? How was it managed?

For many of us, these formative years contain the roadmaps of how we currently feel, albeit at an unconscious level. If you are often annoyed, but don't know why, or break into rages at little or no provocation, the roots of these behaviours may well lie in your childhood. A meaningful chat with a close relative may be very worthwhile.

We have two sides to our brain, the left and right. The left side of our brain is largely thought to control our conscious functions like speech and language, while the right side is believed to be more about unconscious processes such as recognising danger or creating our emotions. Through interacting with others, our brains learn to adapt and grow the neural connections needed for us to survive and thrive. Children who are isolated from others do not develop as well as those who have plenty of access to positive relationships with adults and children alike. Children who are under-stimulated tend to have less brain activity than those whose environment is rich and full of wonder.

It's important that a childminder, if you have one, gives your child plenty of one-on-one attention, but if their house has little to stimulate your child, it is far from ideal. Stimulating environments and stimulating interactions with a responsible adult or parent tend to cause dopamine to be produced in your baby's brain. This is the ideal we should strive for.

The right-hand side of the brain grows more quickly than the left, meaning we hear children develop speech after the first 18 months. The brain growth at this time is focused on attachment and emotional regulation, so how we play with our children and what we show them through our faces is crucial for the toddler's developing sense of self. If parents look disgusted, unhappy or sad to see their child, its developing brain will store this information as a 'truth' about itself and the resultant adult will have feelings of low self-worth and shame.

We interpret each parental facial gesture as evidence of our lova-bility. Playing games with your baby stimulates neural growth both in your baby's brain and in your own brain. Both brains are flooded with dopamine and other opioids that allow a stronger connection to be forged between you. Taking a bath together, bouncing on a bed or even a massage all contribute to forming attachments and making the child feel more secure.

The brain governs the creation of our emotions. Emotions are how we have learned to discern if something is positive or neg-ative. When my child walks towards the open fire and she hears an alarmed sound from her father, she understands that perhaps this isn't a good idea. Internally she may feel fear, stress or shame. According to recent research, it seems that the right side of our brain is orientated towards negative emotions while the left side is where more positive feelings are experienced. The right side is slightly more dominant than the left, hence we might be predis-posed to being unhappy rather than happy. Happiness, it seems, requires more work.

The ability to calm ourselves down when we are stressed is called 'affect regulation'. This is the ability to be happy with ourselves, to feel that we are in control and to have appropriate emotional reac-tions to our environment. The amount of positive physical contact your parents had with you in your early years increased your ability to manage your emotional self. Being able to sit through a difficult business meeting, being able to ignore the flirtatious secretary who just started in your office and return instead to your wife, are all aspects of affect regulation.

If your parents were physically cold, distant or physically abusive, this will have had a serious impact on your ability to handle stress and regulate yourself. Where parental affection was withheld from us, many of us turn to drink, drugs or illicit sex as these release chemicals in the brain similar to those we would have received from a close loving bond with our mothers. Being able to think about our long-term goals, rather than our short-term gratification, may also originate in these early childhood experiences. This is the reason most addicts can't see beyond the weekend.

## THE IMPORTANCE OF TOUCH FOR THE DEVELOPING BRAIN

Touch plays an important role in bonding with our children due to the complex nature of skin. Skin has two types of sensory receptors with differing functions. When we pick up an object, our skin senses if it is hot, cold or sharp. That's a basic survival function. But the other type is dedicated to 'communicative emotional touch'. This is where we interpret the touch as loving or threatening. How we hold our partners and children or how gently we caress them; these actions send messages to the brain that either releases stress chemicals or positive arousal chemicals. This is why baby-massage classes and even adult-massage classes are so popular. We can't get enough of being touched. It feels so good.

To develop fully as a person, a baby needs to know that she can be comforted properly by her parents. This means that she can internalise experiences such as:

- Being caressed until she's calm
- Being held securely
- Feeling the warmth of her parents' skin
- Being fed properly and allowed to sleep when needed
- Gazing at her parents and having the gaze reciprocated

Each of these experiences has the possibility of releasing positive chemicals in our brains that lay the roots for our ability to handle stress in later life. If we find it hard to trust others, or to be physically intimate with someone, the origins of this may lie in how we were loved ourselves. The more loving embraces we received, the stronger the connections are between the various neural networks in our sympathetic nervous system. It's possible that early disruption of the baby's nervous system through repeated separations from the mother can lead to mental illness in later life. Certainly in my experience a great deal of depression has its roots in my clients' earliest experiences. The real challenge is trying to get the background information from their parents about these first three years in order to make sense of it all.

For most of us, the only way we can know if early childhood was stressful for us, is by looking at how we treat ourselves. One of my clients, Fintan, was a barrister who worked about 80 hours per week. He was always stressed. He never felt that he was working hard enough. His senior partner was a bully who frequently put him down. Fintan came for help because his marriage was falling apart. In the course of therapy, he revealed that his father was a very explosive man. His mother was driven by her career and so had little time for nurturing or play. As a result, Fintan was cared for by a series of nannies. While each nanny did their best, they couldn't compensate for the unpredictability of Fintan's parents. He was an anxious child as a result. In school, he tried hard to be top of the class, in the hope this would give him the love and acceptance he craved from his parents. This seldom happened.

When he got top marks in his exams, his parents would turn on him and demand to know how many other children got the same grade; in other words, dismissing the value of his efforts. As a husband, Fintan was cold, distant and prone to violent outbursts, just like his father. It seems that unless we can acknowledge and come to terms with our childhood legacies, we may be doomed to repeat them.

Therapy consisted of giving Fintan the opportunity to speak openly in a safe space about his experiences, and allowing him to acknowledge the overwhelming sadness he carried through having felt unlovable. We then engaged his professor with positive affirmations and worked on reducing his gorilla activation through mindfulness and exercise. Eventually, Fintan was able to see that he was a lovable man, worthy of affection and respect from his wife. He came to realise that life didn't have to be a struggle, and that his wife was his friend and not another mother figure, hell-bent on rejecting him.

## VICARIOUS EMOTIONAL RELEASE

Claire was an interesting client. She was about eight when her parents split up, just as Claire's mum was having a second child. Claire was both delighted and traumatised at the same time, delighted to have a sister but traumatised that her parents were splitting up. When she came for therapy, Claire had two children of her own, one was six and the second had just turned eight. Claire had no problems herself, she confided, it was Sally, the 8-year-old, who was the problem. Sally was getting into trouble in school and refusing to do her homework. She was giving Claire 'backchat'.

In the discussion about Sally, I started to ask Claire about her own childhood. I'm a family therapist so this is what we do. It took a while, but eventually Claire revealed that her own parents had separated when she turned eight, so my questions went as follows:

- What was life like when your parents split up?
- Who looked after you?
- Where did you live?
- Who did you prefer living with, your mum or dad?
- Who gave you support?
- What was school like at this time?
- Did you have many friends in school?
- What was it like to have a new sister?

- What emotions did you feel predominantly at this time?
- Did you cry often?
- What other family members were nice to you?

Claire started to cry as she recounted what life had been like when she was eight. She had been close to her father. He had an affair about the time that Claire's mum got pregnant. There had been a large amount of stress in the house before the split and it was heart-wrenching for Claire each week going from her mum's house to her dad's small apartment. She struggled to keep up in school. She would spend hours looking out the window, wishing it was all a bad dream.

As a child, Claire never had the opportunity to process this situation properly. Her mother and father were too busy with their marriage breakdown to give her the time and support she needed, so Claire buried her feelings instead. Yet here she was now, reliving the pain of her childhood by taking her frustration out on her daughter. She now realised that her daughter turning eight had triggered memories of what life was like when she was the same age. It was very unpleasant.

Claire wasn't sleeping properly and was waking up with a knot in her stomach and a sinking feeling she couldn't shake. This was Claire's unconscious becoming conscious. Her gorilla was sensing fear and distress for no reason. Her thermostat was increasing her blood pressure and putting her in a state of alert. Without any conscious awareness, she was over-critical of Sally and cold towards her. This was causing Sally to act out in school as an attempt to draw attention to the problems at home.

As is often the case with families, brains are closely linked to one another and each has a huge impact on the other. Every little gesture, inflection of voice or stunted affection between us has more meaning than people perceive. Claire eventually came to grieve for the loss of her childhood and in so doing was able to tune into her daughter's needs more effectively. She had to get in touch with her own feelings of loss and sadness first, before she could permit her own daughter to enjoy her childhood.

## TRANSFERENCE

The term 'transference' describes what happened to Claire. Cozolino defines it as 'reacting in a manner inappropriate to someone in a present situation … a distortion of reality of the other based on our past experience' (Cozolino, p. 133). If you have ever met someone and taken an instant dislike to them, that's transference. If you have ever gone to a presentation and decided you liked the presenter before you heard them speak, that's transference.

The unconscious brain processes facial recognition faster than you realise. It also compares the face to a catalogue of previous faces you have met and stored in your memory. Like a computer, it scans to see if you like this face. Some tests have shown that people can react to a face without ever having a chance to consciously see it. Angry faces were flashed on computer screens so fast that the subjects didn't see them, but yet their amygdalae reacted strongly to the images.

The face is an important place for us to direct our attention. We discern if a stranger means us harm or good. Faces give us information, both by the movement of muscles and by unconscious reactions like pupil dilation or blushing. Mentalists who ask us to think of a number are using pupil dilation, among other things, to 'read' us. The eyes are the windows to the unconscious.

Parents gaze at babies, and babies gaze at parents. Each brain is flooded with endogenous opiates as a result. We come to know that looking deeply into someone's eyes is a way of bonding with them. Pupil dilation also makes us look more attractive to the opposite sex, and in the past women used drops of belladonna to stimulate their pupils. Restaurants dim the lights so that our pupils dilate, and therefore we may find our date more attractive. (They also help this process by trying to give us lots of wine.)

Some people theorise that we have a third eye, a 'chakra', that allows us to read people more effectively if we just know where to look. Personally, I tend to look above the eyes when I'm reading people. The forehead area and the eyes give me valuable information. I can discern trustworthiness and stress in this area so when someone is speaking, I have a good idea if they are stressed by what they are saying. Frowns appear when we are stressed and the eyes tend to narrow, to block out light. This may or may not also indicate that lies are being told.

When couples are speaking to one another they should be looking directly at their partner. Too often we shout upstairs, or stand behind someone, making it impossible for them to read our faces. When we go on a date, we tend to want to see the person's face. Why should communication in a long-term relationship be any different?

Where parents have poor eye contact with their children, it can lead the child to fear direct gaze from others. They may believe that being looked at is shameful. We see this when we speak in a group setting and feel everyone looking at us. Positive eye contact from our parents can make this experience less daunting. When someone looks directly at us, there is activation in the gorilla, the insular, frontal and temporal cortices. When someone you find attractive or threatening looks directly at you, you will feel this shift inside yourself. Prolonged gazing at someone may not always be wise. We have to be very selective when we do so, such is the power of the gaze.

When children speak to their parents, the most important response a parent can give is to look with affection at the child. Too many of us are watching our smartphones and feel annoyed by interruption from our children. We frown at them and say 'What?' rather than engaging with them lovingly. I have done it myself and it's a horrible thing to acknowledge that I valued a video of a cat or a dog more than a chance to bond with my daughter.

On the other hand, the more time children spend reading screens instead of faces, the more deskilled they are becoming at the most important skill of all: communication. Without being able to discern if a face is angry, tense, anxious or sad, our children will not be attuned to the emotional needs of those around them, and as a result their ability to bond and form meaningful attachments will also deteriorate. Researchers have demonstrated that recognising emotions from facial expressions uses the right somatosensory cortices. We do this by making an internal map of our own experiences that allows us to intuit what others are feeling.

Survival is key to understanding why the brain functions the way it does. We need to know if a person is a threat and whether we should approach or avoid them. If we approach, what level of bond should we form with them? Should we work with them, sleep with them or befriend them? If we work with them, we need to trust them and agree a way of cooperating with them. If we want to sleep with them, we have to attract them; if we want to befriend them, we need to know how to mirror their behaviour. Then we need to know how to communicate with each of these people to make sure our needs are met from our relationships with them.

Fear, trustworthiness, disgust, sadness, happiness, joy and surprise are the emotions that all tribes and races share no matter where they live on the planet. These are the basic building blocks of relating. If we can recognise these in others, we have a great chance of surviving with them. Problems begin where our ability to read these emotions in others is affected by how life has treated us. If we were beaten as a child, we may not trust others sufficiently to work well with them. If we were never played with as a child and allowed to experience fun, we may be stuck with depression for most of our lives. Our duty as parents is to give our children as many opportunities as possible to experience the full range of these emotions but, more importantly, to teach them how to recognise these emotions in others.

As we mature, our ability to recognise the emotional states of others becomes more developed and sophisticated. The inner Sherlock plays a role in developing an awareness of what others may be feeling. Tests have shown that when we watch someone being rejected in a film while being monitored under an MRI scanner, there is activity in the inner Sherlock. The same brain areas light up when we experience physical pain, which is why there seems to be a correlation between how often married people are physically unwell and how often they feel rejected in the marriage.

One area we seldom explore as parents is how often our unconscious issues may be affecting our children. I had a friend called Peter who had a daughter who was about eight when I knew her. Mum and Dad were separated and, while I knew them both, I was only really close to Peter. Whenever Fiona, the daughter, would pay a visit to my house, she would stand behind her dad's legs and appear terrified at the sight of me. I'm not *that* ugly so I struggled to understand what this reaction was about. As my friendship with Peter deepened, he confided in me more about his own childhood. He came from a loving, warm, supportive family but at school he had never felt like he belonged. He was a highly intelligent student, and was envied by his peers. They mocked him daily, eventually shattering all his confidence in himself. He came to detest school and especially sports, where his classmates had ample scope to ridicule his lack of athletic ability. Without realising it, Peter was telling his daughter that the world is a scary place. Trust no one, they are all out to get you, and you're better off with me.

I happened to meet Fiona a few weeks later but this time with her mother. She was chatty and extroverted, just like her mother. Peter was unwittingly passing on his neuroses to his daughter. If we don't gain awareness of these neuroses, many parents will do this.

## HAVE YOU SEEN MY CEREBELLUM?

How do you think you would feel if you realised you were missing part of your brain? Okay, that question must look like a mistake, but it isn't. In 2015, doctors in China discovered that a woman who had been complaining of dizziness was missing her cerebellum, a crucial brain part that plays an important role in speech and language formation, movement and coordination, and also in one's social behaviour. 'Primary Cerebellum Agenesis' was first discovered in 1831 and only nine cases have ever come to light, this being one of them.

The Chinese woman in question had some slight impairment of speech and walked in an unusual manner but was able to marry and at the time of writing had a healthy daughter. This is another fascinating example of neurological adaptation. The cerebellum was originally only thought to be involved in coordination but now we believe it has a more social aspect, too. Isn't it fascinating to think that someone can be missing a brain part but not even know? How many marriages are in trouble because one or both partners have faulty brain wiring? Should brain scans be mandatory before marriage? Perhaps!

How well do you think you relate to others? Are you sensitive to their feelings? Do people like to be in your company, or not so much? One of the most important skills any parent can impart to their child is the skill of being liked. When I hire people to run my marriage courses, I hire them using likeability as a key factor. I can train someone to be a great speaker, but I can't train them to be likeable. They either have it or they don't. What most of us don't realise is that a part of the frontal lobe called the orbitofrontal region, which is located just above the eye, hence the name, if developed properly helps us to respond well to other people and therefore become more popular.

Another part of the same brain region, the ventromedial area, facilitates us in becoming more aware and makes us better negotiators. If we have strong connections from this area to our lower brain, we are better able to handle difficult emotions. We are able to reason with ourselves and calm ourselves down, rather than letting emotion take over.

The way your parents interacted with you as a child formed these connections for better or worse. The more encouragement you received, the more praise and social rewards, the stronger these connections became and the more social skills you developed. Children who grew up believing that they weren't liked by their families tend to feel that they are unlikeable. When one member of a couple feels unlikeable, it places a huge strain on the relationship. As you can't change your past or your childhood, what can you do to repair these brain areas and make yourself more likeable? Most neuroscientists agree that this is where long-term therapy may well be needed. Dan Siegel believes that long-term therapy, with the right therapist, can replace the missing original parental relationship and cause changes deep within the brain structure that allow clients to learn to love properly once more.

For Siegel, the quality of the relationship between client and therapist is more important than the qualifications or level of training of the counsellor. Certain brain areas can form new connections within the limbic system once the client experiences unconditional positive regard, empathy and understanding from the therapist. For some clients, the release of oxytocin and dopamine during body-work sessions, where the therapist uses therapeutic touch to heal, can compensate somewhat for the lack of affection in their early childhood experiences.

At the start of this chapter I asked if parenting could cause brain damage, the inference being that parents can experience profound changes in their brain structures that may well be considered a form of brain damage thanks to the stress caused by parenting. But what about parents themselves, can they unwittingly cause brain damage to their children? If so, might some of the issues that you face with your partner today stem from his or her childhood? Is it time to (reluctantly) blame the parents?

A number of bestselling books suggest some controversial solutions to the difficulties associated with parenting. Take, for example, the problem of a baby who can't (won't) sleep. Some parenting advice about a baby who 'refuses' to sleep seems simple: leave the baby cry itself to sleep. Do not touch or console the screaming baby. Do not relent and soothe the baby, ever. It may take two months of listening to your baby scream for comfort, but stand strong and do not yield. Eventually, we are told, the baby will realise that no one is coming and will stop wasting its time by screaming. Thousands of parents have read these books. In 20 years' time, thousands of neglected babies may enter adulthood with brain damage.

What kind of brain damage are we talking about here? Well, a baby who is left to cry for extended periods will experience huge surges of cortisol, the stress chemical. This can lead to high levels of fearfulness and irritability. These children can become over-vigilant in attempting to read the non-verbal signals of their closest caregivers. High cortisol levels in infants is also linked to obesity, alcoholism and eating disorders in adults, as these adults find it difficult to regulate their emotions. Before I was a family therapist, I worked with children in care homes who as babies were neglected by their parents. As young pubescent children, some had lost muscle mass and failed to grow; others couldn't regulate their emotions and were violent to other children and staff.

The impact of neglect on children is severe. To cope with prolonged exposure to cortisol, the baby's brain will eventually shut down the cortisol receptors. This is known as 'down regulation'. These children seem to be unaffected either by happy or sad stimuli, but wear a veneer of happiness all day instead. Low cortisol may be associated in later life with physical abuse and aggression. Neglected children can make very unhappy spouses. If you are married to someone who seems distant, shut down, emotionally flat or, on the other extreme, is frequently raging or violent, the roots of this behaviour may well be in how they were loved or unloved by their parents.

Other babies who were neglected by their parents suffer from 'alexithymia', the inability to name one's emotions. I often have clients who don't know how they feel. When asked, they tell me that they feel 'fine' or 'okay' when they would have been expected to feel angry or upset. So the next time you hear a parent tell you that they leave their baby cry itself to sleep, consider saying something, you might just be saving a brain.

## WHERE DOES YOUR PERSONALITY COME FROM?

There is no doubt that genes play a role in a child's temperament; however, in his book *How Not To F\*\*k Them Up*, Oliver James makes the point that more of a child's personality is determined by the interplay of environment, chance and family dynamics than we realise. Two children born into two different families but with similar genetic dispositions may have very different life trajectories. In one family with a low socio-economic status, the child with a gentle and timid disposition growing up in an urban environment, surrounded by poverty and gang culture, may not thrive. Another child with the same type of disposition growing up in a salubrious area may fare much better.

How parents encourage or limit children's beliefs also plays a huge part in their future development. If the economically deprived parents are warm, loving and responsive to their child, he or she may well achieve any amount of success. Contrast this with the child of the wealthy parents whose parenting style may be distant, unresponsive to their child's needs, and uncaring. The supposedly 'lucky' child may end up with chronic substance-abuse issues or an eating disorder. Many rehabilitation centres and psychiatric hospitals are home to the teenagers and adults of wealthy but unresponsive parents.

Sometimes parents make the mistake of over-praising their children. When this happens, children can start to believe that they are invincible. Eventually, however, the child discovers that they are not as fast, artistic or as creative as their peers. This can lead them to doubt what their parents tell them in future. Getting the balance right between nurturing conversations and giving meaningful feedback is the key to helping your child gain a strong self-concept. It can do more harm than good to praise them without good reason: telling them you love them is more important than telling them they are geniuses.

## WHERE DID YOU COME IN YOUR FAMILY?

Where you come in your family has an impact on personality development. We know that eldest children are often over-responsible, over-controlling and more stressed as a result of parental pressure to achieve. Youngest children are often spoilt, attention-seeking and under-responsible. Middle children don't quite know their place in the family so tend to stay quiet and become the peacekeepers.

Parental expectations, too, are a bigger influence than we might first think. I have only one daughter, and probably won't have any more children. So do I dress her only in pink, do I give her only dolls to play with or do I encourage her to take up martial arts or become a DJ when she is three? ('Three,' I hear you say, 'she can't be a DJ if she's only three.' Oh yeah? Look on YouTube for the videos of a 3-year-old boy mixing dance music. His name is DJ Arch Junior, and he is incredible.) All these decisions by her parents will have a bearing on who she becomes. (I want her to be a DJ. It has been decided. Just don't tell her mother I said that.)

What happens to the parents during the child's early years also plays a part in shaping the child's personality. If after having a baby you are unfortunate enough to lose your job, the stress from this event may affect how much time and attention you're able to give your baby. The death or illness of your own parents can equally impact on how you relate to your child. If you're told that your son or daughter looks like your father-in-law, a man you can't tolerate, this may leave an unconscious impression on you that impacts on how you treat them. Genes have a much smaller role in personality than we want to admit.

## THE EARLY YEARS

Our beliefs about our own self-worth came from our interpretation of how much we were loved, and we measured this in the amount of quality time we received from our parents. I have met many people who grew up in abject poverty, with five or six siblings competing for attention, who are now multi-millionaires because, despite everything, they always knew they were loved and their parents had instilled in them a 'you can do it' mindset.

The more love we received as children correlates to the amount of compassion we can feel for others. Using MRI machines, researchers have been able to see which area of the brain is involved in compassion: the anterior cingulate cortex (inner Sherlock). By sculpting your child's brain with love and affection, you can help to create strong connections between their higher brain and their lower brain. In doing so, they will have more empathy for others. If the cerebellum and the frontal lobes have strong neural connections, those children are better able to communicate, to negotiate with others and to resolve conflict.

Put simply, your ability to relate well to your partner was formed decades before you even met each other. Even our ability to read proxemics (the art of managing personal space) correctly was shaped by the quality of connections between the parietal and frontal lobes. So men or women who continually 'get in your face', or feel the need to be pushy or aggressive, may well suffer a deficiency in this important brain area.

If you or your partner is prone to impulsiveness or making rash decisions, then this may well be caused by low serotonin levels. Early stress in a baby's life can lead to low serotonin; the importance of keeping your baby calm in the early years is vital for how well they can relate to others in their intimate relationships later in life.

The lack of forethought that lies behind much of our addictive behaviours and the associated risks people take as gamblers or sex addicts have at their roots a lack of serotonin at the times in the child's life when it was most needed.

One of my clients was on the verge of a nervous breakdown when she came to see me. Sabrina was a young, energetic woman with a demanding job. Her boss had recently spoken to her about her intimidation of colleagues. Sabrina was a leader of a sales team and her commission was linked to the performance of her team members. To motivate them, she had used one-to-one sessions with each team member where she effectively bullied them in quite a sinister manner. A number of complaints had been filed against her as a result. She was in serious trouble and was close to losing her job. In the course of our consultation, Sabrina admitted that she was used to getting her own way, and that bullying other people came naturally to her. In fact, it was the reason that her husband had left her two years previously. The first thing I did was to investigate what life had been like for Sabrina as a child.

Sabrina was the youngest of three children. Her parents were under a great deal of stress when she was born, being stretched both financially and emotionally. Sabrina's arrival was an unwelcome surprise. Their parenting style was to criticise her and make unreasonable demands of her; nothing she could do was good enough for them. Frequently, her mother resorted to smacking her when Sabrina was slow to comply. Shouting and raging around the house, her father was not much better. While he didn't hit Sabrina, he had a habit of shaming her whenever she made a mistake or failed at something.

Sabrina was able to trace her own behaviour in work back to her childhood. She became aware that she lacked empathy and warmth for her team because she had seldom experienced these at home. She was using shame and guilt to try and coerce her team into better performances, rather than using more effective methods such as praise and team-building experiences.

In Sabrina's brain, as in the brains of many bullies, the connections between the frontal lobes and deeper brain parts were not formed properly. Adrian Raine, the British psychologist, has scanned the brains of murderers and found deficiencies in the higher brain areas. The professor, which acts as our executive brain, was not working properly in the majority of his subjects. In many cases, he discovered that these murderers were victims of appalling childhood experiences themselves, involving parental violence and neglect. As a result, they lacked empathy and compassion for others.

The statistics for domestic violence throughout the world are truly shocking, with millions of men and women affected. In my opinion, if we are ever to curb this damning social issue we need to better educate parents about the enormous impact they can have on children and invest properly in early childcare that has been fully grounded in neuroscientific principles.

## GENIUS: NATURE OR NURTURE?

Would you marry someone you didn't love, and didn't know that well just to prove a theory? Matthew Syed in his brilliant book *Bounce: The Myth of Talent and the Power of Practice* first introduced us to Laszlo Polgar. Polgar married his girlfriend Klara at a registry office in Hungary in the mid 1960s. Polgar was an educational psychologist in the process of testing a theory about whether genius came from nature or nurture. Klara, who had been seduced by his charm and enthusiasm for his project, agreed to marry him, and to give birth to his child, all in the name of science. Klara was a young Ukrainian who had been in contact with Polgar for a number of months by letter before meeting in person. Once they were married, the experiment duly began.

Polgar believed that talent was not inherited in one's genes. He believed that a person's success was more to do with the environment they grew up in, the encouragement they received and how the parents interacted with their child. On 19 April 1969, their baby girl, Susan, was born. The experiment was now in full flow.

Polgar wanted Susan to be excellent at something, he just wasn't sure what. He eventually decided that chess would be her specific area of expertise. Why chess? He chose chess 'Because it is objective, if my child had been trained as an artist or novelist, people could have argued about whether she was genuinely world-class or not. But chess has an objective rating based on performance, so there is no possibility of argument.'

Polgar, not a professional player himself by any means, spent hours and hours teaching Susan about chess. He let her handle the carved wooden pieces when she was a toddler. He brought her to see chess tournaments when she was just four years old, where she would sit on her father's knee enraptured by the competitions unfolding before her eyes. By the time she was five, she was hooked. At her first tournament, Susan was so small that she could barely see over the table but, undeterred, she played on. Susan won ten games in a row, aged just five. Her opponents were all at least twice her age. She was marvelled at by parents and children alike.

By January 1991, Susan had become the first woman player to be given the title of Grandmaster. By the time she finished her career, she had won the women's world championship four times and became the only person in history to win the Triple Crown, which consisted of the rapid, the blitz and the classical world championship. Although an expert chess player, her path to success was not easy. Susan had faced sexism along the way and was prevented from entering championships because of her gender. She persisted and now runs her own chess centre in New York.

Klara and Laszlo eventually had two more daughters, Sofia and Judit. They, too, were taught to play chess by their father, with support from their mother. Sofia's accomplishments included winning the Magistrale di Roma, where she won eight straight games against many of the greatest male players of all time. Sofia is seen as one of the most influential chess players in the world and now runs a chess website. Judit is currently the world's number one female chess player; she is considered to be the greatest female player of all time.

So Klara and Laszlo, who by all accounts married purely for the sake of Laszlo's experiment, were able to create not one but three children who developed extraordinary skills and acumen that ultimately changed our perception of the nature versus nurture debate forever. But these parents were not alone.

What do Michael Jackson, Venus and Serena Williams and Tiger Woods have in common? Besides their ethnicity, all four were parented by determined and focused parents; some would say obsessed parents whose belief in their child's future stardom was unwavering from the moment they were born. In the case of the Williams sisters, before they were even conceived, their father Richard had been surfing the television channels and happened upon a presentation of a cheque being given to a female tennis player for forty thousand dollars, an enormous amount of money at the time. Right then and there, Mr Williams decided that this was going to be the sport his children, if he ever had any, would excel at. The rest, as they say, is history.

Were all these children loved extensively and parented exceptionally by their parents? Not always and certainly not in the case of Michael Jackson. He was regularly beaten by his father Joe and singled out for special treatment, of the unpleasant kind. The young Michael was also expected to achieve more than his siblings. That may have accounted for some of his intense drive to succeed. So if his toddler's brain did not receive the essential love chemicals that children need, how did he manage to do so well?

Michael was surrounded by people who loved him and believed in him. His extended family of aunts, uncles and grandparents were able to show Michael regularly that he was loved. In their own way, they helped him maintain the sense of self-worth that is essential to success. His brain was likely flooded with oxytocin and dopamine from the applause he received at his early performances for his family, and this would have fuelled his desire for more.

The brain will always adjust to its environment and make the most of what it has. The concept of compensation is an important one. Just because we don't feel loved by our parents does not mean we don't feel loved. In many cases, we are capable of internally repairing the damage done by bad parenting once other loving adults are available to us. Thankfully, our brains are constantly growing.

History is filled with stories like this, of parents who 'hothoused' their children to incredible success. In every case, the prodigies share common traits. They had the opportunity to practise extensively at their chosen field, their parents were dedicated without fail to their training or preparation, they themselves loved the experience of training or practice and they developed an internal desire for success that was independent of their parents.

We usually assume that musical ability is a trait you either have or don't have. Not true. Musical ability is learned. In studies of the world's most successful violinists, to take one example, it was found that each had spent literally thousands of hours in practice. Malcolm Gladwell in his book *Outliers: The Story of Success* informed the world that the magic number is ten thousand hours of practice, about ten years, in fact, to become an expert in your field. If you as a parent decide you want your child to be exceptional at something, there's every possibility this may happen, if you really believe it's possible. Your self-belief is as important as your child's, and if you both put in the huge effort it takes to reach those heights of brilliance, then yes, it can happen.

So we have established that genius can be created in addition to possibly being inherited. But are there negative consequences to trying to create a genius? According to Oliver James, one of the risks of this style of parenting is the possibility of creating anxiety and depression in our children. Stephen Fry and Elton John, brilliant entertainers, suffer significant bouts of depression and even suicidal tendencies, which they say are the result of demanding and critical parents. As we have seen, the ability to regulate our emotions, and to self-soothe when we are in distress, are essential skills we must develop. By receiving constant criticism from our parents, we end up doubting our own self-worth. If we are raised in a stressful environment, where nothing we do is good enough, then our gorillas are over-sensitive to clues from our environment that we are under attack, even when no attack might be imminent.

One of the best ways to guarantee your child's success, at sport, at least, happens before they're even born. Malcolm Gladwell charts how important the 'birth month' is for sports stars in *Outliers*. He found that the majority of very successful sportspeople were born in December. Why so? Very simply, if you were an under-16s soccer player who was born in December, then you would be almost twelve months bigger and stronger than your teammate who was born in January. This extra strength and weight would confer on the child a very real advantage over everybody else. As a result, they were more likely to be singled out for extra coaching, and this in turn increased their skill set in that sport.

## HOW TO CREATE A GOOD HABIT

When we learn a new skill or habit, numerous brain parts must work together in sync to give us some degree of mastery. Take piano playing, for example. I bought a keyboard last year for a moderate sum of money. It sits in my sitting room. Occasionally I tinker on it, usually playing along to songs on Spotify that I like. I have a good ear for music and can bang on the right keys at the right time in the correct manner to follow along with the tune in question. This is my very conscious brain at work. However, in order to learn chords, and then to be able to play those chords without looking, a number of other brain parts must activate.

According to Elkhonon Goldberg, clinical professor of neurology at New York University School of Medicine, 'the process of habit formation on the basal-ganglia level is also two dimensional. It is characterised by a gradual transition of neural control from the right dorsomedial reward centre to the left dorsolateral reward centre' (Goldberg, p. 226). Put simply, for a habit to become a habit, either good or bad, the part of the brain that has conscious control must give up that control and let the unconscious brain take over. This never happens within your awareness. It just happens.

Matthew Syed tells the story of going up against a famous tennis player for a charity match. Being a world-champion table-tennis player, with lightning-fast reflexes, he figured he had a good chance of at least returning the serve. He watched his opponent toss the ball high in the air, saw it being hit by the head of the racket, then, suddenly and scarily, the next thing he was aware of was the sound of the tennis ball passing close to his ear, at what turned out to be 125 miles per hour. He had never even seen it. How could this be?

How could a world-class table-tennis player be unable to see a moving tennis ball?

The problem was in his brain. His brain had not yet figured out that in professional tennis, one doesn't look at the ball or the racket, but at the movement of one's opponent's upper torso. From here, professionals are able to discern where the ball is likely to go. It's called 'chunking', i.e. taking snippets of information and deducting probable outcomes from the bits of information you gather. Successful people do this all the time, and in every field, even in business. Can neuroscience help you in this process? Unfortunately not, all it can do is reiterate the importance of the thousands of hours of practice it takes to make a conscious skill unconscious.

## SCREEN TIME

Neuroscience can, however, educate us about parenting. For example, thanks to brain science we now know that children under two should never watch television. If they do, they tend to copy what they see, good or bad. An experiment took place where children were put into two groups. One was the control group and the other was shown a television show for 20 minutes. The control group did not watch television but played with toys. After the allotted time, both sets of children were observed carefully. Those in the control group continued to play as before, with no change. The children who had watched TV began mimicking what they had seen, including quarrelling and pushing one another.

Studies have found that for every hour a child watches TV (under the age of four), the risk of bullying behaviour increases by 9 per cent, by the time they enter school. The reason is deferred imitation.

By the time a child is 18 months old, she can imitate an event four months after a single exposure to the event. This skill never leaves your child. Before I knew this, I allowed my daughter to watch Wimbeldon for about five minutes of an evening. I marvelled as she raised her own tennis ball to serve, in unison with Roger Federer. In fact, your child is encoding values, beliefs, behaviours and norms for their adult lives based on what they see on TV, online and within their parents' relationships.

How many children's TV shows encourage children to listen to their parents and do as they say? My guess is not that many.

Children who watch cartoons are being saturated with the message that violence is okay. The vast majority of children's cartoons depict animated creatures in power struggles in one form or another. Some experts estimate that a child will have seen ten thousand acts of violence by the time they are eight. When watching violence in cartoon form, a child's gorilla will activate as it registers fear and confusion in line with the content of the cartoon. The toothbrush is also jumping to life, carefully watching the actions of the creatures on TV and sensing which, if any, are useful for the future. It's still a surprise to many parents that their children become angry when they try to limit their TV time.

Perhaps the anger is being generated within the child from watching the programmes themselves, as few cartoons depict cooperation, reasonable thinking and dialogue as positive values. The thermostat, which regulates our overall well-being, will release chemicals in your child's body to increase their heart rate and breathing in response to the frenetic activity on screen. Hence it's difficult to remove children from TV and then expect them to sit still and eat dinner. They can't: after an hour of television their adrenaline and cortisol levels are through the roof. And that's just from cartoons.

The more our children watch violence on TV, the more they imitate it in real life. When people commit acts of violence that are viewed hundreds of thousands of times on Facebook or YouTube, it gives a precedent to other people to behave in the same way. Mirror neurons activate in group-think situations where one person throws a punch, and then five or six friends also join in.

A prison warden I interviewed from Dublin's Mountjoy Prison told me that the majority of his clients were chronic gaming addicts. Frequently, fights would break out in prison when wardens tried to limit gaming time. (What types of games were they playing? *Call of Duty* and *Grand Theft Auto* were favourites.)

Television and gaming are fast becoming the least of our worries, for those of us concerned with the cognitive development of children. Every time I visit a coffee shop (you know the ones with the nice brown leather chairs and a woman's face in the logo), I am shocked by how young the children, no, the babies are that are being given smartphones to play with.

When children grow up exposed to tablets or smartphones, they lose valuable neural networks that encode metadata from our environment, in particular other people's faces. As a result, psychologists are seeing an increase in autism and cognitive development issues. I have interviewed a number of primary-school teachers who have complained that it is now virtually impossible to keep young children engaged in any task for more than five minutes. Concentration spans are dwindling, and creativity in children has declined as a result of smartphone and tablet usage. There is some evidence that children's brains are being rewired towards technology. Some children are developing ADD and ADHD as a result of excessive exposure to technology. When in doubt, remember the saying, 'Everything in moderation.' If you see your children becoming zombified, take them away from whatever screen they are watching and give them a book to read.

## SMACKING

Children have three hungers: for stimulation, recognition and structure. It is the adult's responsibility to ensure that these hungers are met, and, when they aren't, a toddler will sometimes throw a tantrum. When we smack children, we activate their gorillas and instil fear in the child's brain. This over-activates the gorilla, which makes our child very stressed. To alleviate this stress, the child may start smacking their parents, other children or animals. Children imitate what we do. Our job is to offer them 'best practice': hitting them isn't it!

My aim in this chapter was to show that many of the interpersonal issues we face today have their roots in our childhoods. We can't change the past but we can choose what to focus on when we look back over our lives. If we look for the positives in our life experiences, we will do ourselves more good than if we only focus on what we didn't have. Learning to accept the past can allow us to accept ourselves with compassion, and this in turn can make us more tolerant of our partner's flaws. Nobody is perfect.

# 9

# THINKING OUTSIDE THE BOX

Is the Brain Lazy?

A Ball and a Bat

Biases

## You Saw the Whole of the Moon

A great many people think they are thinking when they are merely rearranging their prejudices. – William James

Thinking is probably one of the most important activities we can engage in. If we could just learn to think more effectively, our lives would improve greatly. We would be more positive, more focused and perhaps more reasonable to live with. Thinking properly could even change how we view the world.

Take, for example, heliocentricity. For centuries, we believed that the sun revolved around the earth. In 1543, that illusion was shattered when Nicolaus Copernicus asserted that the earth revolved around the sun, and not the other way around. He not only asserted it, but through rigorous experimentation was able to prove it. In doing so, mankind had to fundamentally change its perception of heaven, hell and everything in between.

Most of our important scientific discoveries have involved changes in thinking, be they perception or judgement. Yet throughout history our best scientists and philosophers always held the belief that their view of reality was the 'objective truth', much like how we perceive reality today.

Not if you are a constructivist philosopher like Heinz von Foerster. Constructivism is a relatively new branch of epistemology that asserts that we can never know reality for what it really is.

Von Foerster believes that we create reality as much as reality creates us. It's a bit of a stretch to understand this but let me give you a concrete example that you may relate to. Next time there is a vivid full moon in the sky, take a long hard look at it. Observe the relative size of the moon to the landscape around you. In an hour or two, look at it again. Has the moon become smaller or bigger? Has it changed colour, become clearer or blurry?

My guess is that you will 'see' a different moon. But the moon can't possibly have changed size, shape or colour so what's happened? The truth is that your perception of the moon, thanks to the light hitting your occipital lobes in various different light waves, has altered your perception of the moon's colour and size. You are essentially 'imagining' the moon all by yourself. In fact, everyone sees the same moon differently, depending on how their brains interact with the light waves in question. Reality is a co-construction between your brain and the universe itself. No one sees the same world as you.

So what's the relevance of this for you? Well, next time you're convinced your perception of your partner's 'misbehaviour' is the correct one, pause for a moment. What if it's wrong? What if your emotions are affecting your perception? Worse still, what if your ability to 'perceive' is less reliable than you imagine? Truth is, it might be.

One of George W. Bush's first major international incidents as president of the United States involved a submarine and a fishing boat. On 9 February 2001, only a month into his term, a submarine commander onboard the nuclear submarine USS *Greeneville*, stationed off Hawaii, ordered a surprise manoeuvre known as 'emergency deep', where the submarine suddenly dives. This was followed by an order for an 'emergency main ballast blow', where the submarine rises quickly to the surface. You have probably seen this manoeuvre in films like *The Hunt for Red October* where the front of the submarine heaves right up out of the water. The commander, Scott Waddle, was in for a bit of a shock, indeed the entire crew was. The submarine surfaced right under a Japanese fishing boat, the *Ehime Maru*. The submarine sliced through the fishing boat like a knife through butter, killing three of its crew members and six passengers.

During the subsequent investigation, various reasons were put forward as to what might have happened. Perhaps Scott Waddle was distracted by the civilian tour he'd had to accommodate on his submarine? Maybe it was a technological failure in the submarine's sonar systems?

Waddle used the ship's periscope just before he gave the order to surface, so should have been looking straight at the *Ehime Maru*, yet he didn't see it. Why not? He didn't see the fishing boat because he didn't expect to see it.

## THE THREAT RESPONSE

Amadou Diallo was a 22-year-old dark-skinned man from Guinea living in the Bronx area of New York. On the night of 4 February 1999, Diallo was hanging around outside his apartment, essentially minding his own business and not bothering anybody. However, to four plain-clothes police officers driving by, he looked suspicious. Two of the officers got out of their car and approached him. They were wearing baseball caps and bulletproof vests so they must have looked like the kind of men that you don't want to stay around to chat with, so he didn't. Like what most people scared out of their wits would do, he ran inside the apartment building. In the melee that followed, two of the officers later testified that they saw Diallo reach for something in his pocket so they screamed at him to show them his hands. 'Don't make me fucking kill you' is how one of the officers responded, in fact.

Tensions mounted as Diallo, who had poor English and a stutter, still refused to engage in a dialogue with the officers. They saw him pull something black from his pocket, assumed it was a gun and began to fire off shots. This brought the other two officers who had remained in the car into the building where they experienced a noisy and dangerous shootout between Diallo and their colleagues. Diallo hunched down in one of the corners of the vestibule where he was positioned, giving further proof to them that he was making a deliberate attempt to avoid being arrested. Over 20 bullets were discharged between the four officers in those few moments. None of them were from Diallo.

When the officers approached his lifeless body, riddled with bullet holes by this point, they searched for his gun. What they found instead was his wallet. He had been trying to show them his identification to prove he wasn't a threat.

A number of important changes were happening in these men's brains before they chose to run after Diallo. This is called the 'threat response'. In this situation, the gorilla triggers a response in the hypothalamus. This activates the pituitary gland, which secretes adrenocorticotropic hormone. Epinephrine is also released into the bloodstream at this time. Cortisol is then produced, which increases blood supply around the body preparing us for fight or flight. Once the threat has been fully perceived, working memory starts to be affected by all the chemical changes inside us. Working memory helps us to think clearly. Memories of similar situations are scanned by the brain to see if the current scenario fits any previous experiences and what lessons can be taken from them. The frontal lobes are particularly affected by the threat response, meaning that concentration and rational thought are much more difficult.

Diallo's brain was saying, 'Get out of there, these men are going to kill you' (the flight response) while the police officers' brains were probably saying something like, 'This guy looks suspicious, you better investigate to see if he's dealing drugs or about to rob someone' (the fight response). Neither response was correct but our brains are designed to get us out of trouble, fast. Waiting around to see what happens is not an option.

Stress or fear affects our perception of the events taking place around us. If we can't think accurately, we can't react to situations appropriately. When this happens, we spiral out of control and tend to 'catastrophise' – we assume things are much worse than they really are, just like the four plain-clothes police officers that fatal night in New York. While driving around that dangerous neighbourhood their stress levels were so high they misread Diallo's intentions completely and saw a threat where none existed. They opted to fire first and ask questions later.

## THE INVISIBLE GORILLA

In *The Invisible Gorilla* by Christopher Chabris and Daniel Simons, the authors give a description of a (by now) world-famous experiment they conducted that drew on the work of the psychologist Ulric Neisser. They set up two small teams of basketball players wearing different-coloured bibs, and recorded the players throwing basketballs to one another. They then asked their subjects to watch a video of the event and count how many times the players wearing white bibs threw the basketballs to each other.

Most subjects studied the video carefully and gave accurate answers. Some, however, failed to notice the man dressed as a gorilla who walked into the centre of the basketball players. The gorilla looked straight at the camera and beat his chest for over seven seconds. In fact, almost half the subjects didn't see the gorilla even though it was right there in front of them. After they were told about the gorilla, particpants accused the experimenters of trickery. They still refused to believe there had been a gorilla, and suggested that the video had been digitally altered instead.

The experience of not seeing objects that are clearly in your field of vision is known as 'inattentional blindness': 'When people devote their attention to a particular area or aspect of their visual world, they tend not to notice when those unexpected objects are salient, potentially important, and appear right where they are looking' (Chabris and Simons, p. 7).

The gorilla experiment is thus a demonstration of the 'illusion of attention' whereby 'We experience far less of our visual world than we think we do' (*ibid.*). In fact, we believe that everything that happens around us is noticed by us, and that any significant events will be remembered by us exactly as they happened.

The truth is much murkier. We often see what we want to see, not what's there. We often experience what we believe we should experience, not what's really happening. The context that we find ourselves in often dictates how much of the world we perceive accurately.

## THE ILLUSION OF MEMORY

According to Chabris and Simons, 'memory doesn't store everything we perceive, but instead takes what we have seen or heard and associates it with what we already know'(*ibid.*, p. 48). I no longer trust the recollections of my clients, or give them the status of 'fact'. I now appreciate that when it comes to memories, 'we cannot easily distinguish between what we recall verbatim and what we construct based on associations and knowledge' (*ibid.*).

When it comes to our relationships, we can safely assume that some details of our previous arguments are fictional. Yet we trot out past arguments over and over again to prove our point, embellishing the details as we go, to fit our narrative at the time. Thanks to fMRI scans, we now know that women remember far more details from previous arguments than men do. There's just no proof that the details they remember are as accurate as they think they are.

If you met Bugs Bunny at Disney World, you'd remember, right? Elizabeth Loftus is a memory expert who wanted to see if memories could be implanted in our minds. She created an advertisement that showed some people meeting Bugs Bunny in Disney World. She showed the advert to people who had visited Disney World and asked if they too had met Bugs Bunny while there. In fact, it turns out that 25–35 per cent of her respondents had met him, 62 per cent had shaken his hand while 46 per cent recalled hugging him! They could never have met him, however, as he is a Warner Brothers character and Disney World is owned by Disney. What this proves is that memory is fluid, malleable and unreliable.

Marriage expert John Gottman cautions against using past arguments to illustrate how right we are in our current arguments. Bringing up past issues only inflames the current ones, making it impossible to separate out the hurt caused by the current issue from hurt from the past. As we have seen, there's a more important reason why you should never bring up past arguments: they may never have happened in the first place, at least not the way you remember.

Nietzsche claimed that 'There are no facts, only interpretations.' When we retrieve a memory, we are using two specific brain areas: the medial temporal lobe (MTL) and the frontal parietal network (FPN). The MTL works on the specifics of the event, the FPN works on the overall gist of the event. When we remember an event such as 9/11, we can remember vividly where we were and who we were with. These are known as *flashbulb memories*. They are memories that have a significant component of emotion attached to them. 9/11 is remembered mostly for the sheer terror it caused in us all. Was this the beginning of the Third World War? Are we safe? What's going to happen to civilisation as we know it?

In other countries around the world, large buildings are regularly blown up by opposing armies, on a daily basis, in fact. Entire cultures are eradicated during some wars but we don't remember these events. Why not?

We don't remember them partly because we don't see them. 9/11 was unique in world history in that we had hundreds of hours of footage on television channels shown around the clock of the same tragic events. This meant that we had repeated exposure to the same feelings caused by the initial viewing of the attack on the Twin Towers. The fear we felt had plenty of opportunity to embed itself in our brains, and embed itself it did. Post-traumatic stress rates soared in the aftermath of 9/11, not only in those physically affected, but in those who couldn't stop watching the footage on TV.

We know that memories can be implanted. We also know that powerful emotions such as fear or anger can strengthen our memories of events. But can we reduce the power of painful memories? Can we, in effect, rewrite history?

You may have heard of visualisation, the process sport stars use to imagine making that kick or sinking that putt. I use this process with my own clients but in reverse. In order to displace the traumatic impact of a negative experience that may be blocking the client from reaching a goal or attaining happiness, I use a system I call 'reverse re-imagining'.

John was a 50-year-old sexual-abuse survivor. John was abused by his uncle for more than three years while he was a young teenager. When he came for therapy, he was angry, frustrated and ashamed. He believed that he should have been strong enough to fight off his uncle, despite being just a young boy.

After three years of therapy, I knew John had placed his trust in me so I asked him if he felt ready to recreate his childhood. He was curious so he agreed.

I began by dimming the lights and inducing a mild hypnotic-like trance in John. We focused on his breathing for about 30 minutes and made sure he was fully relaxed. Then I asked him to recall a painful memory that was still troubling him today. He began speaking about an incident where he had been abused in his uncle's kitchen. He had felt overcome with fear and felt stuck to the floor so he couldn't escape. The abuse continued for a few minutes and afterwards he cried alone in the dirty alley behind his uncle's house. He remembered it was just after his twelfth birthday because he was still wearing his 'I'm 12 today' badge.

I then suggested the following 'ideas' to John. 'John, I want you to imagine this for me as best you can. You're in the kitchen with your uncle. He looks at you and asks you to come over to him. But then you say out loud, in as loud a voice as you can manage, "No, I won't, I don't want to, and you can't make me!" At this point you run outside and run straight back to your parents' house where they comfort and support you.'

We did this exercise for a few weeks together, each time giving John different opportunities to feel empowered. We varied the response he gave his uncle to include pushing the uncle away, and calling for help from a neighbour, to running outside and bumping into a patrolling policeman. Eventually, John settled on the recreation that felt most plausible to him and so we 'implanted' this memory into his mind.

Months later I was speaking to John about his childhood and asking him to identify times in his life when he felt a surge of pride. He recalled one occasion of being alone with his uncle in his uncle's kitchen and his uncle trying to abuse him. He remembered grabbing a frying pan from the counter top and hitting his uncle between his legs, causing him to buckle over in pain. I asked John what he felt after he had done this. He remembered going outside to the alley and feeling elated that his uncle would never again have power over him, or cause him fear or pain.

This incident never happened. It was John's new 'implanted' memory. Today, John is a successful journalist and author.

## COGNITIVE DISSONANCE

Leon Festinger developed the concept of cognitive dissonance in 1955. This is the name given to the trouble we have hearing information that does not fit our preconceived view of reality. Dan Gardner notes in his book *Future Babble: How To Stop Worrying and Love the Unpredictable* that 'the human mind wants the world to make sense. For that to happen, our cognitions – our thoughts, perceptions and memories – must fit together' (Gardner, p. 200). Numerous experiments have confirmed that even when faced with overwhelming evidence that contradicts our perception of an event, we still prefer to cling to our version of reality.

Kerry and Lawrence were together about four years when I met them. Kerry was close to her sister, too close, according to Lawrence. The sister, Anne, lived with the couple but refused to pay rent. Kerry didn't push the subject because she felt sorry that her sister had no job and no place to live. Lawrence believed that Anne was lazy, selfish, manipulative and calculating. In their sessions together he recounted story after story of Anne's misdemeanours. Kerry was having none of it. As far as she was concerned, Anne just needed their support. Nothing Lawrence could say about Anne had any impact. Anne could do no wrong. Eventually, the couple decided to separate.

When we are 'wedded' to a belief about something, no amount of contradictory evidence makes a difference, especially when the belief in question threatens one of our core values. Take faith, for example.

I once had a customer complain that I was using a quote from Bill Cosby in one of my pre-marriage workbooks. (At the time of writing there are allegations in the media about Bill Cosby's sexual misconduct with a large number of women.) I thanked her for her input but I also asked if she was aware that the hierarchy of the Catholic Church, in which she was marrying, and to whom she would be giving a sizeable donation, continues to facilate the physical and psychological abuse of thousands of women around the world, according to the United Nations and others.

She didn't seem happy to hear this; perhaps it didn't fit with her romanticised view of getting married in a church and all that she imagined this would entail.

When we argue with our husband or wife we generally tend to feel vulnerable. This means that our self-concept is fragile. The worst thing to do at this point is to cause your partner to experience cognitive dissonance. You could do this in a number of ways. You might tell him that he's lazy, or ignorant, or stupid; any insult, really, that contradicts his view of himself. Should you do this, he will become extremely defensive and his brain will work overtime to right this wrong and find evidence of his opposite characteristics. He will then counter-attack with either a defence of his own virtues or an attack on yours. Neither will make either of you feel any better.

We seldom like to hear that the world is not the way we think it is – just ask Copernicus, who quickly discovered how unpopular his ideas were. We cling to our beliefs. They allow us to navigate our world safely.

## IS THE BRAIN LAZY?

We prefer to be in 'lazy relationships' – in other words, when our partners conform to our current needs we experience cognitive ease, but if they challenge our needs by changing our daily routines, for example, or adopting different beliefs to ours, we tend not to like it. We have billions of basal ganglia that control our routines and they like things to be just so.

'Cognitive ease' is the experience of feeling content and safe in the world. It's the belief that you are right about whatever issue is being discussed. You know what's what.

You come home from work, sit down and relax. You have achieved your monthly targets and your bank account is about to receive a nice bonus. Your mortgage is up to date, you have no debts, all your family are happy and well. Then the front door opens and your wife arrives. Her face is flushed and she's clearly angry. In your mind you start to think, 'What have I done wrong, did I forget something she asked me to do?' Cognitive ease has just been disturbed and depending on how emotionally mature you are you may or may not be able to calm her down. If she decides to have a go at you over something trivial, in her attempt to distract herself from the real source of her pain, you have a choice about how you react. Reaction A: tell her to go and jump; Reaction B: tell her you love her and ask her if she wants a coffee. Which do you think takes the most effort?

At times, we like to simplify our behaviour and that of the people close to us into frames of reference that make sense to us. In the case above, the husband may choose to think, 'Oh here she goes again, flying off the handle at nothing,' or he might think, 'My poor wife, obviously something terrible has happened, I hope that I can help her.' While such simplification may be understandable, it may not always be wise.

As humans we are prone to be influenced by what the behavioural economist Daniel Kahneman calls 'heuristics', 'a simple procedure that helps find adequate, though often imperfect, answers to difficult questions' (Kahneman, p. 98). Take biases, for example.

A bias, according to Kahneman, is a 'systematic error that (System 1) is prone to make in specified circumstances' (Kahneman, p. 21). In other words, it's an inbuilt tendency we have towards simplifying difficult problems into meaningful answers, despite how wrong they might be. To demonstrate, I need a ball and a bat.

## A Ball and a Bat

Kahneman sets us the following simple puzzle. Do not try to solve it, as such, just let your intuition go to work on it.

> *A ball and a bat cost $1.10.*
> *The bat costs one dollar more than the ball.*
> *How much does the ball cost?*

If you said the ball cost 10 cent you would be wrong, yet this is what most people have said when faced with this puzzle. If the ball costs 10 cent, then the total cost will be $1.20 (10 cent for the ball and $1.10 for the bat. The correct answer is 5 cent. The incorrect answer was given to you by your System 1, but you really needed to engage your System 2.

Kahneman informs us that we have two distinct systems operating in our brains all the time.

He defines our two systems thus:

- System 1: operates automatically and quickly, with little or no effort and no sense of voluntary control.
- System 2: allocates attention to the effortful mental activities that demand it, including computations. The operations of System 2 are often associated with the subjective experience of agency, choice and concentration (Kahneman, pp. 20–1).

In our everyday lives, we are only ever aware of one of these systems, System 2. It's this system that's reading these words, trying to assess their relevance and deciding whether to keep reading or not. System 2 is what we define as our personality. System 2 decides what to eat, what to do and where to go.

System 1, on the other hand, is where our automatic responses originate. Driving, skateboarding and surfing are all System-1 activities. To have to think about what you're doing while driving or surfing could be fatal. We could never stop and process those activities, they are automatic and unconscious. System 1 contains many of the brain areas that we met in our quick guide to the brain in Chapter 3 and is incredibly complex.

We are born with an inbuilt fear of snakes or spiders. Evolution has encoded System 1 with special knowledge and abilities to get us out of danger whenever necessary. Our amygdalae will sense danger and respond immediately; we don't have to wait for System 1 to figure it out, thankfully.

System 2 demands more energy from us than System 1 does. Think about doing some of the following activities:

- Recall a memory of a frightening sound you once heard
- Count how many times I say 'System 1' in this page
- Compare the value of your current car to your last car using current depreciation levels
- Write down five telephone numbers from your contacts list and text them to a friend

Can you see how much more taxing it is to use System 2? The activities above use a considerable amount of energy. When it comes to arguing with our partners, who wants to sit down and 'think' during a row? But to keep our biases under control, that's exactly what we have to do.

Kahneman (like me) argues that each of us is lazy and that inevitably we will suffer from what Keith Stanovich calls 'lazy' thinking.

Stanovich and his colleague Richard West have been studying what makes some people more prone than others to biases of judgement. In Stanovich's book *Rationality and the Reflective Mind* he gives System 2 two separate skill sets: 'algorithmic' and 'rationality'. While perfectly intelligent people may be able to do higher-order mathematics, have incredible memories and so on, it also means that some intelligent people are just as prone to biases of judgement as those with lower IQs, as we saw in the ball and bat problem.

In other words, no matter how bright your partner is, there's no guarantee that when it comes to 'thinking', he or she is any better at it than anyone else. You might be right after all!

## Biases

Biases play important roles in how we perceive and manage reality. We use them to interpret complex social situations and to simplify such situations for us. Meeting many different people at the same time can be stressful. If you go to a large family occasion with relatives all milling around you, one of your biases may be 'People I like, people I don't like'. This allows you to allocate the limited time you have available to the people you like the most. This assumes, however, that everyone you like likes you in return. If you start chatting to some of the people you like, but they seem disinterested, the next time you meet them, your bias will kick in and you may put these ungrateful individuals into the category 'People I don't like'.

We do something similar when it comes to our love relationships. Our toothbrush, which is largely responsible for our unconscious habits, is encoded as follows: 'If X, then Y'. Or, to translate: 'If he comes down the stairs and complains about the dishwasher not being emptied, I will remind him that I work 60 hours a week whereas he only works 35.' Not the wisest response, I hasten to tell you, but it may 'feel' like the right response.

We are fundamentally lazy beings. We like to think we know how to relate to our partners and that this doesn't involve a huge amount of effort. As a result we often struggle when the automatic processes of System 1 are no longer effective. When your girlfriend or boyfriend does or says something that you disagree with, you have a choice: either say something or stay quiet. If you choose to say something then your System 2 is going to have to work hard to navigate your way through the ensuing argument. Many of us therefore say nothing. This has its own drawbacks – including resentment. Resentment is a very dangerous emotion. It's almost always permanent. By the time one person acknowledges that they feel resentment there is usually no way back. The damage has been done.

Below is a brief summary of other biases that may affect your perception of reality – see how many you identify for yourself and how they might apply to your relationships.

- Anchoring bias: You hear a piece of information about a subject and you give more weight to it over anything else you hear, because it was the first thing you heard.
- Availability heuristic: You overestimate the importance of the information available to you, rather than look at the facts, e.g. a smoker will think, 'Well, I know three people who smoked all their lives and they were just fine,' rather than look at the actual facts of cancer deaths.
- The bandwagon effect: The more people that hold a belief, the easier it is for you to hold to that belief too and never question it.
- Blind-spot bias: Failing to identify your own biases is a bias in itself.
- Choice supportive bias: When you choose something, like a new boyfriend or girlfriend, you tend to ignore flaws in the relationship, because you chose them.
- Clustering illusion: The tendency we have to see patterns in random events that have no connection to one another.
- Selective perception: Allowing our expectations to influence how we see the world – when we are feeling angry we only see our partner's flaws, not their strengths.

## WHAT IS CONJUGAL COGNISANCE?

'Conjugal cognisance' is the term I use to explain how some couples fail to see reality for what it is and adopt the same world view as each other, rightly or wrongly. It is a form of bias that puts the couple into a 'them' versus 'us' situation. Let me give you an example from my own practice.

Donald and Rita came to see me about six years ago. They were having problems with Don's family. Don came from a wealthy family. He was in his fifties when he married Rita and was due to inherit the family wealth once his frail mother passed away. She was 85 and needed full-time care. This was provided by a combination of family members and a team of professional nurses.

The problem was that Don didn't think that it was his role to help out in the care of his mother, despite the fact that he was the person who would gain the most from her wealth. Rita concurred. She appeared in the sessions to be more interested in isolating Don from his family than helping him connect. This surprised me and for a few months I couldn't understand it.

Eventually I broached the subject with her. I asked her directly if she had more to gain from keeping Don separate from his family or connected to them. Rita explained that she was adopted. Growing up with no real sense of identity or feeling of belonging, she was incredibly threatened by Don's family who were, by all accounts, enmeshed – they were close and were in touch frequently. Her family were disengaged – she rarely saw them and she never shared intimate details of her life with them. Only her brother attended her wedding, and even now she rarely spoke to him.

Don was in love with Rita so he didn't want to upset her. Instead he changed his world view to match hers. Despite my interventions, Don moved further from his siblings and by the time his mother died, they seldom spoke at all. It seemed that conjugal cognisance had taken over.

## THE FATHER OF PUBLIC RELATIONS

Edward Bernays was the nephew of Sigmund Freud and is regarded by many as the founding father of Public Relations. At one point in his career, he was commissioned by a powerful lobby group for American farmers. His challenge was to make sausages, bacon and eggs: a staple American meal.

Bernays knew the value of 'social proof', a term made famous by Robert Cialdini, the author of *Influence: The Psychology of Persuasion*. Social proof is the weight we give to a concept because other important people have given it value before us. In this case, Bernays contacted hundreds of American doctors and had them write letters of approval along the lines of 'I, Dr Steve Medic, give my full backing to the benefits of people eating bacon, eggs and sausages as their main breakfast food. This combination will give you all the nutrition you need to have a happy and productive day.' Bernays then paid newspapers to carry this story on a regular basis, supplemented by half-page adverts for said items. Within 20 years his strategy was successful, and he had managed to convince millions of Americans to follow this carcinogenic diet (the World Health Organization stated in 2015 that it is likely to cause bowel cancer if eaten regularly).

Today we can frequently observe this PR exercise in operation with regards to alcohol. Numerous media reports tell us that drinking wine on a regular basis could help prevent heart attacks or strokes. This is not actually the case: there is little evidence whatsoever that drinking alcohol regularly is beneficial to us. Alcohol is a poison. Like any poison, the body and brain has to work hard to get rid of this toxin. Anything other than that fact is pure spin.

A significant number of couples drink a bottle of wine every night of the week, and more at the weekend. You might be one of those couples. If so, due to conjugal cognisance, it will be difficult to acknowledge that this is a problem. Together you will convince yourselves that this is normal, and given that your friends may do likewise, the bias known as 'group think', combined with conjugal cognisance, will keep you both trapped in an alcohol-filled haze. I was one of those people who occasionally enjoyed too much wine until I stopped drinking completely two years ago. About three months after I stopped drinking, I decided to approach a publisher. I had always wanted to write a book but without my knowing it, alcohol had been robbing me of creativity, motivation, focus and drive. Thanks to my sobriety, you are now able to read this book. What projects have *you* postponed? Is it time to reclaim your natural brilliance once more?

## PATTERNS

From our earliest days on the planet, trying to predict the weather, or when a volcano was likely to erupt, we tended to see patterns in everything. 'At times, we perceive patterns where none exist, and we misperceive them where they do exist' (Chabris and Simons, p. 154). Some anthropologists believe that many of the great world religions we have today were man's attempts to make sense of the difficulties of living with and controlling nature. Early priests told villagers that they could predict when it would rain and performed rituals to that effect. Witchdoctors were equally in vogue because they helped their tribes make sense out of seemingly random events such as sickness, death and unhappiness.

Let me ask you some questions. Who was born on 25 December, to a virgin called Mary? Whose birth was accompanied by the appearance of a star in the east? Who was a prodigal child teacher at just 12 years of age? Who was baptised when he was 30 and then began his ministry? Who had 12 disciples supporting him in his work? Who performed miracles such as walking on water? Who was crucified in his early thirties but three days later rose from the dead? Did you answer 'Jesus Christ'? Most people do.

But another answer is Horus, the Egyptian Sun God, worshipped a thousand years before Christ. In fact, the same mythological sequence can be found for over 20 other gods, such as Attis, who was worshipped in Greece 1,200 years before Christ. Krishna and

Buddha also shared many aspects of the same sequence of events. Was this a coincidence? Hardly!

The reason these stories are so similar is because early man watched the movements of the sun very carefully. To understand the winter equinox, where man experienced the shortest, and therefore the most frightening, day of the year, early man created a story to help explain what was happening. The sun was buried but, three days later, rose again. This is a reference to the shortest day of the year. The 12 disciples are in fact the 12 constellations in the sky. Mary was Virgo, and so on. To explain how the planet worked, mankind throughout the ages has created mythological stories to give us some sense of control and comfort. (For more information on this topic, I would like to refer the reader to search YouTube for a documentary made by the Canadian Broadcasting Corporation called *The Pagan Christ*, based on a book of the same name by a former Anglican priest, Tom Harpur).

When a couple is in crisis, each scans the partner's behaviour to find evidence that their negative view of them is justified. This gives each individual more reason to disengage from finding solutions. This pattern-recognition mechanism is essential to our survival; however, when we are going through difficult times, it can be unwise to trust the patterns we seem to recognise.

An entire branch of therapy called solution-focused therapy aims to stop this. It asks couples to find exceptions to the patterns they believe exist in their partner's behaviour. So when a man tells me that his wife is always insensitive and hurtful, I will ask him to recall a time when she was neither hurtful nor insensitive. In doing this, I am moving his inner Sherlock in a different direction. Through associative ideation he will then start to remember other times when she was supportive and we can build on that.

In 1970 Edward de Bono wrote, 'The mind is a pattern making system. The information of the mind acts to create patterns and recognise them.' He states that 'if you offer a random arrangement of lines to a group of people they will soon start to pick out significant patterns' (de Bono, p. 27). If you find that you're unhappy with your partner, for whatever reason, you may find meaning in their actions where none exists. For example, you have an argument during breakfast and at 7 p.m. you receive a call to say that he/she will be late home from work. These are two totally separate incidents but if you're angry or upset then you may see one causing the other. An argument is likely to ensue.

Derren Brown once did a visual experiment to prove our need to find patterns in life. He put a group of people into a room filled with an array of toys, gadgets, balls, hoops, etc. Above one of the walls was an LED counter. He told the group that their job was to figure out how to make the LED score higher. But be careful, he warned them, some of their activities might make the score lower!

They began in earnest. One man jumped on a spacehopper and started to circle the room. The score went up. Another woman rang a bell: the score went down. Another jumped on a pogo stick: the score went down. After 30 minutes of attempting to influence the counter, Brown asked for their feedback. What was the secret pattern that could increase the score?

They gave him their long-winded assessment of how to control the LED counter and were convinced they were right. The only problem was that nothing they did actually had any impact on the score, it was going up and down completely at random. They had 'intuited' a pattern that did not exist. Much like we do in our relationships, we see patterns of behaviour that fit our belief system and we 'force' reality to conform to our viewpoint, be it right or wrong. This is known as confirmation bias. If we are stuck in a rut, only seeing the negative traits of our beloved, it's very hard to see the good in them. We prefer to fall back on our own bias: it's altogether easier.

Confirmation bias keeps us locked in conflict because we sometimes fail to acknowledge that our view is not the correct one. Rather than adopt a flexible thinking approach that allows for multiple perspectives, we prefer to root ourselves in our own biases. This seldom works.

## LATERAL THINKING

There are two important types of thinking that can help your relationships: lateral and systemic. Both can make important contributions to resolving arguments and thinking clearly.

It was de Bono who first coined the term 'lateral thinking' back in the 1970s when referring to a way of conceptualising answers to problems that we commonly call 'thinking outside the box'. Our education systems do not readily teach lateral thinking; they teach vertical thinking, which means dealing with problems head-on. De Bono's systems are far more inventive and creative. Take a pen, for example. What is a pen to be used for? We know it's to write with, but is that all it can be used for?

De Bono encourages students to brainstorm multiple answers to these types of questions. The pen could be used as a door wedge, or as a weapon, maybe as a secret listening device like in a James Bond movie. He calls this the 'generation of alternatives' model.

When my clients tell me a story in therapy sessions about how a lover, friend or family member has done something they are unhappy with, I usually ask why they think the person did the action in question. Most of the time clients answer with a personal angle: 'They did it to annoy me'; 'Because they're insensitive'; 'Because they're thoughtless', etc. At this point, I have them brainstorm other possible reasons based on de Bono's model. You would be amazed how useful this process is for helping people reframe reality and develop new perspectives. Then clients say something like, 'Well, he might have been stressed'; 'She might not have slept the night before'; 'He might have been feeling insecure'. This opens the way for clients to feel differently about the person or situation causing the problem.

The second strategy we are taught as part of lateral thinking is 'challenging assumptions'. De Bono gives the following challenge as part of his training. A man worked in a tall office building. Each morning he went into the lift on the ground floor, pressed the button to the tenth floor, got out of the lift and walked up to the fifteenth floor. At night he would go into the lift on the fifteenth floor and get out again on the ground floor. What was the man up to?

Some of the explanations given have been:

- The man wanted the exercise.
- He had a friend he wanted to chat to on the way up.
- He liked to look at the views on the way up.

In fact, the man was a dwarf and couldn't reach higher than the tenth-floor button in the lift.

In practical terms, when faced with a problem in your relationship, the worst thing that you can do is to assume that the view you have formed, because you have formed it, must be the correct one. It's vital that you both discuss your assumptions about the issue and then challenge each assumption you come across. None may be true. Alternatives do exist. Your duty is to find them.

The third strategy of lateral thinking is called 'looking for the dominant idea': 'Why are we always looking at this thing the same way?' (de Bono, pp. 112–13). In doing this we give ourselves time and space to wonder what principles govern our beliefs. This process is very useful when you are both in a good space and can take the time to listen to each other's views on the topic or issue in question.

## SYSTEMIC THINKING

The next significant thinking practice that can help both partners in a relationship is called 'systemic thinking'. Most of us go through life thinking that A causes B. There is no more to the equation than that. Systemic thinking challenges this assumption. It asks what if A caused B because B needed A to cause it, and if A didn't cause B, then perhaps C would have stepped in instead. Confused? Let me explain.

Kevin and Lacy were Americans who had recently moved to Ireland. They had two children, a boy aged 6 and a girl aged 13. When they came for therapy they brought their children with them, which I always like to see as it gives me different perspectives on the same problem. The session started with the parents complaining that they felt their children had no respect for them. Kevin was quite loud while recounting stories of the kids' attempts to thwart his authority. He blamed both children for his stress. Lacy sat there nodding and agreeing with everything Dad said. Both children looked quite unhappy.

At this point I asked Simone, the daughter, why she thought Dad looked so angry in the session. She replied that maybe it was because of work. She told me that Dad was on the verge of losing his prestigious job in a multinational here in Dublin. Kevin disagreed strongly at this point, saying his job was safe and that he would never let his children see him stressed, anyway.

I then brought Lacy into the conversation. I asked her the following questions:

- What would the kids have to do differently to ensure that there were no more arguments in the house?
- If the children didn't exist, what would you as a couple argue about?
- Were the children happier living in the US?
- How much time did they have to adjust to the idea of moving to Ireland?
- Did they have any choice in the matter?
- Did you as a couple have any choice in whether to move to Ireland?
- What do you do for fun?
- Do you have friends here in Ireland?
- When Kevin is at work, what do you do to fill the time?
- How much exercise does each person in the family get each week?
- What is your diet like?
- How are you finding Irish food?
- When is the next family holiday planned for?
- Have you been in touch with the family members you left behind?

- Are the children happy in their schools?
- Is there a long commute to school?
- On a scale of one to ten, how happy were the kids in their schools in the US?
- What number would you give them for how happy they are in school today?
- When was the last time that you told the children that you loved them?
- When was the last time that you praised both children for being good kids?
- When was the last time that you both spent individual time with them?
- When did you last have a date as a couple?

As you can see, these questions are opening out different possibilities as to why the children are not accepting Dad's authority – if that's even the case to begin with.

We learned that the children were stressed because their new schools were an hour away from home, and they had no friends there yet. Their diet was appalling. Junk food and processed food was the norm. They were feeling bloated most of the time and the teenager was beginning to feel self-conscious. The parents would probably have argued about money if they didn't have children. Kevin wanted Lacy to get a job but she was too nervous about going back into the workforce, especially in a different country where she knew nobody.

The parents seldom told the children that they loved them, and neither parent spent individual quality time with either child. Mum acknowledged that Dad was stressed at work and it was nothing to do with the kids but that he probably wanted to feel more in control at home, given how little control he had at work. This meant that he became demanding and authoritarian, which was unlike him, and the kids didn't know how to handle him. She admitted that she was anxious herself as a result of his temper tantrums.

Kevin's thinking went something like this: 'I'm stressed because my children will not behave themselves.' Introduce a systemic lens on the same situation and we get a different perspective, involving all members of the family feeling stressed for different reasons.

In practice, we need to be open to the idea that there are multiple realities or lenses that can give you insight into any of your problems. In staying open to this idea, you will navigate your problems more effectively, and remove blame from the equation almost entirely. Blame, as John Gottman notes, is another of his marriage busters, and needs to be avoided at all cost.

Some systemic questions that you can use to help your relationship include:

- What do we, as a couple, want to achieve over the next 3, 6 or 12 months?
- How would we know we have achieved these goals?
- What areas of personal or interpersonal growth should we focus on this year?
- What behaviours do we need to eliminate from our interactions?
- What sayings, phrases or statements have we experienced to be hurtful and are we committed to removing them from our relationship?
- Are we clear about our goals in relation to money, sexuality, communication, social activities, wish fulfilment and romance?
- If a miracle happened overnight, and our relationship was perfect in every way, which of us would notice it first and what exactly would we notice?
- Is there anything that we are doing very well as a couple?
- How can we do more of these actions or activities on a daily, weekly, monthly basis?

## CANCEL THE SHINK – BREAK OUT THE CHOCOLATE

The next time you feel like saying something you know you probably shouldn't, make sure you have some food handy. Better still, make sure you have two bars of chocolate in the fridge, one for you and one for your partner.

Eating chocolate releases endorphins in our brains, and leads especially to an increase in phenytlethlamine. This makes us feel more alert and excited. Chocolate even produces some dopamine in the brain and another compound, anandamide, which has a similar impact on the brain as marijuana, so it calms us down. When we eat chocolate, theobromine is released, which acts on the brain in a similar way to coffee. The best type of chocolate to keep in the fridge is dark chocolate, at least 85 per cent cocoa. Eating some chocolate while you are in the middle of a row will calm you both down sufficiently to reappraise the issues in a different light. The brain uses up a huge amount of energy, especially System 2, and a ready supply of chocolate can give you both the sustenance you need to make up properly.

System 2 is the mental facility we use to argue but, as I mentioned already, it's exhausting. In practical terms this means that sustaining an argument or listening without prejudice to your partner's issues can be draining. During the argument you may eventually come to suffer from what we call 'ego depletion'. This is where we lose motivation to sustain the activity we are engaged in, e.g. not overreacting to your partner's comments, or, as demonstrated by an expert on willpower, not eating Oreo cookies.

## WILLPOWER

Roy Baumeister is a psychologist with a keen interest in willpower. His book of the same name is a fascinating read and, when applied to love relationships, his research has profound implications, both for adults and children. In a series of experiments, he demonstrated that using our mental faculties to perform complex calculations eats into our reserves of mental energy. By placing a jar full of Oreo cookies on a table and asking subjects to perform complex mental tasks (without eating the cookies), he discovered that our ability to restrain our impulses and not eat from the jar decreased the longer subjects performed the complex tasks in question. Baumeister wondered if the source of our mental energy is, in fact, glucose, a simple sugar. By increasing our glucose levels he found that subjects were more capable of restraining themselves from behaviours they were trying to avoid, and could make complex calculations more effectively.

Willpower, in other words, is a form of sugar. (This is why you should never quit smoking and sugar at the same time; the brain needs sugar in order to quit smoking.) Willpower is also needed to stop couples fighting.

Lee and John had been married for three years when they came to see me. They had met while working in the UK, fallen in love, and were married as soon as they could legally do so. Lee had a habit of saying whatever came into his mind; he liked the fact that he was so 'forthright', as he called it. John had loved this aspect of Lee's personality, too, and, being the shy and retiring type, he felt secure knowing that Lee would always stand up for him.

After the inevitable disappearance of the love chemicals, John began to feel differently about Lee's outspokenness. At John's family occasions, such as the baptism of his nephew, Lee was quick to tell everyone how little he agreed with organised religion. This became a source of embarrassment for John. In their sessions with me, both men were able to verbalise their issues clearly. Lee made an agreement that he would stop speaking out of turn at these events and keep his thoughts to himself. They went away from therapy with a clear plan of action and both men seemed satisfied that progress had been made.

A few months later I had a phone call from Lee. Things had gone badly. After keeping quiet at John's family occasions, Lee would get home and have a huge row with John. This was completely out of character. Neither man could understand what was happening. It then dawned on me that perhaps Lee's willpower was being used up trying to stay quiet at these all-day family events. I asked Lee if these arguments usually occurred before or after dinner. You guessed it: before dinner. Thanks to ego depletion, by the time they got home the normal household issues that he would usually ignore seemed much bigger than they really were. Lee could no longer restrain himself and took it out on his partner.

We seldom think of its importance for happy relationships, but willpower is a key component of long-term marital satisfaction. Your life could be improved in many ways if you only had more willpower. But what do you do if willpower is not your strongest attribute? Can it be improved with practice? Is self-control genetic or learned?

Walter Mischel decided to find out. He created an experiment in Stanford University that would change our perception of will-power forever. He arranged for a number of 4-year-olds to be brought into a room and offered a marshmallow. If they waited 15 minutes until the experimenter returned, they could have two marshmallows. The poor children twisted and turned and tried everything to distract themselves from the temptation. Some stared at the clock, some sang songs. Others gave in right away and gobbled down the marshmallow.

When this experiment took place, in the 1960s, the fact that children could distract themselves was an interesting finding. What was more interesting was what Mischel discovered later. Thanks to follow-on studies with hundreds of participants, he learned that those children who had waited the full 15 minutes were more successful and happier than those children who had caved in during the first 30 seconds. They were also slimmer and earned more money than their less restrained fellow test subjects.

Further studies on self-control indicated that where people had high self-control, they were less likely to get angry, hit their spouses, cause unnecessary arguments or be malicious. They had fewer emotional problems, ate less, drank less and abused drugs less. Overall, people who had high self-control were more happily married than those without it. In 2010, a study in New Zealand tracked one thousand children from early childhood to age 35. Those who had scored highly as children in terms of self-control were wealthier, had better jobs and were more likely to be physically healthy.

In our day-to-day relationships with those we love, it can take willpower to stop ourselves from interrupting mid-sentence. It can also be challenging not to tell them they're wrong, if we believe their construction of reality is erroneous. At other times, for example in public with friends, when your spouse is recalling a tale of woe from your holidays, which you remember in a totally different way, saying nothing can be a challenge. If your husband's 6-year-old niece is misbehaving while on a sleepover and he chooses to ignore it, it can take great self-control not to point out the error of his ways. While it's seldom mentioned in marriage self-help books, gaining self-control is a definite feature of successful relationships.

In the brain, those with high self-control have more activity in their pre-frontal cortex. This is where we think logically, process decisions and recall important information to help us choose our course of action. Those without self-control show more activity in their ventral reward centre, which is linked to short-term gratification. It makes sense when you think about it.

## MINDSET

Carol Dweck is not so sure that sugar is the source of our willpower. She thinks that sugar may become a placebo – a non-medical intervention that we believe to be the source of our cure or recovery, despite having no such properties itself. For her, the mindset we adopt is more important.

Take someone suffering from anorexia. They have low blood-sugar levels and are physically in need of food, but something in their mindset refuses to let them eat. Baumeister discovered that students who believed that they had ample stores of willpower fared much better than those who did not, a form of self-fulfilling prophecy. Does this mean that we can increase our self-control by repeatedly telling ourselves that we have it? Yes, perhaps.

In her book *Mindset: How You Can Fulfil Your Potential*, Dweck reveals that if we choose to be positive, we can achieve far more than if we choose to be negative. The majority of couples in therapy have unconsciously chosen to be either negative about themselves or their relationship. This makes it difficult for the therapist to change either partner's mindset. Dweck believes there are two types of mindset, 'fixed' and 'growth'. In the fixed version, people believe that their intelligence levels were fixed at birth and can't change. The growth mindset takes the view that intelligence, or indeed most of our traits, can be worked on and improved with practice. Dweck found that people with fixed mindsets spent less time trying to solve her tests than those with growth mindsets – *they* believed that eventually they would figure it out, and usually they did.

What do Sarah Jessica Parker and Tom Cruise have in common? They were both raised in less than salubrious surroundings; in fact, they both grew up in poverty. This did not stop them achieving success. Their mindset determined that they would be successful. Michael Phelps, the illustrious swimmer, was dyslexic in school. Richard Branson, who was also dyslexic, hated school so much he left early. Both have had remarkable careers. Mindset is everything.

In other words, if you both choose to have a growth mindset, no issue is insurmountable and any problem can be fixed with time, patience and determination.

## SELF-CONTROL

Numerous studies have confirmed that people with high self-control don't need to rely on their willpower all that much because they set up their lives in such a way as to not need it: 'they're better at arranging their lives so that they avoid problem situations'. (Baumeister, p. 239). Baumeister also notes that such people 'use their self-control not to get through crises but to avoid them' (*ibid.*, p. 239). In practical terms, this means that willpower is best used initially to negotiate the issues that cause you and your spouse difficulty. This is preferable to having to resist the temptation in the first place, be it overanalysing, over-arguing or over-complaining. Take your pick, temptations are everywhere.

It turns out that most people follow Oscar Wilde's adage: 'I can resist everything except temptation.' In Germany, Baumeister tagged hundreds of normal working Germans with beepers. These went off at random intervals. The subjects had to report whether, at the time of the beeping, they had experienced some form of desire, or had recently felt some form of desire. The majority of subjects reported feeling some form of desire when the beeper sounded. The researchers concluded that most people spend about three to four hours of their day trying to resist desire. Those desires ranged from a desire to eat food, drink a fizzy drink, check Facebook or follow inappropriate sexual urges.

Modern life is stressful. By the time you both get home from work, you're exhausted. You have had to bite your tongue all day, saying nothing to that annoying customer or colleague (when all you wanted to do was scream at them). So instead we vent at our partners. We diffuse our rage by attacking the person we love the most about their lack of thoughtfulness when really that anger should have been dealt with some other way. We have used up our willpower; we are a spent force. It's much easier to lash out at our husband or wife. But it's also very bad for our relationships.

## Don't Argue when You're 'Hangry'!

I suggest a different approach. I suggest that before we reach home, we recall just how angry or frustrated we were that day and give ourselves five minutes to think, process and reframe. A reframe is a powerful exercise in reshaping our experiences. If a customer drives you mad, rather than staying angry or frustrated when you reach home, during the five-minute thinking exercise recall something about the incident or situation that you're proud of. Allow yourself to believe that you performed really well at whatever tasks you had to accomplish. It doesn't matter if this isn't true. The point of the reframe is to create a different feeling in your body by the time you open the front door. You need to 'arrive' feeling happy and content, not angry and resentful. Ego depletion is dangerous, do everything in your power to prevent it. Most importantly, don't argue when you are angry *and* hungry, i.e. 'hangry'.

With ego depletion comes another hazard: associative activation. According to Kahneman, 'Ideas that have been evoked, trigger many other ideas, in a spreading cascade of activity in your brain' (Kahneman, p. 51). In practice this means that during a row, with no glucose reserves remaining, you are more likely to recall previous hurts than you normally would. This is also why your emotional responses during an argument are far stronger than maybe you or your partner can understand. If you are physically hungry while arguing, thanks to associative activation you may be linking all sorts of ideas to the emotions being stirred up, with no time to process any of them. The 'cascade' effect Kahneman mentions is powerful: I've seen it happen many times.

To prevent this from happening, it's important to set some ground rules for how you process conflict. My suggestions are as follows:

- Agree to discuss one issue only in any 20-minute period.
- Wait as long as you need to ensure that this issue is resolved fully before discussing another.
- Give each other space and agree that it is okay to 'cool off' as needed.
- Never use examples from the past in current arguments.
- Use your first names as much as possible.
- Do not depersonalise your partner by using the word 'you'.
- Avoid all uses of 'should'.
- Avoid all uses of 'always' and 'never'.

## THE SELF-CONCEPT

Our parents instil in us a sense of our self-worth, especially in the first three years when our brains are going through the process of 'pruning'. This idea of self-concept is what Brian Tracy, the business-success expert, calls the 'most important discovery of the twenty-first century'. Our self-concept is the sum total of all the beliefs that we have about ourselves based on all the experiences in life we have had to date. A strong self-concept means that we think clearly and act more readily in our own best interests. We choose to associate with positive people. We educate ourselves and progress steadily towards our goals. A strong self-concept means that when an argument happens in our relationships, our gorillas don't feel unduly threatened so we react more slowly and thoughtfully.

One couple I worked with had a distinct pattern of conflict that was the result of two unruly gorillas. For over 40 years, this couple experienced life in the following way. Everything would be fine for a few days but then Lorraine would notice that Fred was becoming more agitated from dealing with his intransigent business partner. In noticing that he was becoming more agitated, Lorraine would begin to instigate a process of escalation with Fred. She would tell him that he was agitated. He would try and refute this. In the course of this exchange she would start to shout at him, thereby increasing his stress and making him angry. When she spotted the telltale signs of Fred's anger, Lorraine would leave the house and move in with her sister. She did this every week, for 40 years. By the time they came to see me and get some help, both gorillas were well used to each other's jungle-like rituals. Needless to say, getting their professors onside was quite a challenge.

If we don't learn to think properly, our relationships will suffer. We may assign meaning to actions that aren't true; for example, your wife forgets your birthday and out of nowhere you start to feel unloved and insecure. We might be overly critical of our lover because we think he is critical of us, even though this may be entirely fabricated in our own minds. A distinct form of therapy has been created to help couples with faulty thinking called 'reality therapy'. It teaches couples to think realistically.

When it comes to problems in relationships, mostly it's our partner's behaviour that upsets us the most, not their thinking. Unless they turn into a misogynist overnight or have some other dastardly personality change you didn't predict, their thoughts stay very much in their own heads and don't cause us any concern.

But by the time a couple comes for therapy, the thoughts of both partners are usually starting to show signs of being faulty. In other words, their gorillas are overruling their professors. It's tricky for the therapist to separate out fact from fiction.

A stunning, dark-haired woman sat in front of me recently with her husband, and complained that he didn't spend enough time with their children. My gorilla reacted and said, 'That's awful, what a lazy sod, and with a gorgeous wife like that, you would think he'd make more of an effort.' At this point my professor piped up, 'What do her looks have to do with anything? What if he works 14 hours a day and is just exhausted?' As it turns out, my professor was correct. Levi ran his own company and was working about 80 hours per week. Further exploration with the couple revealed that Levi had no memories of his own father spending time with him; all his own dad did was work. Levi's gorilla was uncomfortable being in his bare feet tumbling around yoga mats surrounded by mums. While his professor knew that dads today do more than they did 30 years ago, Levi still couldn't control his gorilla's reaction to this request from his wife. Gorillas are always more powerful than professors, at least to begin with.

Gorillas are highly emotional creatures. They walk into a room full of strangers and decide immediately who you should speak to. They wake you up in the morning either in good form, bad form, or somewhere in between. They don't like to be wrong and they are easily agitated.

Last week a neighbour's boyfriend, a well-built, tattooed, skin-head chap, partially blocked the entrance to my estate with his car. My professor politely asked him to park it elsewhere in future, pointing out that where he had parked was blocking other neigh-bours' vans from entering the estate. His gorilla reacted, became defensive and started to become confrontational. Mine sprang to life at that point and started to bellow back. After four minutes of heated debate, we each drove away in a rage. I wondered for a long time afterwards if I was physically strong enough to fight him should he have attacked me, and I resolved to work harder in the gym as a result. My professor was quiet the entire time.

When two gorillas are arguing in a marital conflict, it's very difficult for couples to stay connected. Most of us don't realise how powerful gorillas are, or even that they exist! We grow up thinking that we are in charge of our minds and that we have free will. Nothing could be further from the truth.

Gorillas are also lazy. They are prone to making mistakes. One such mistake, as we learned earlier, is 'inattentional blindness'. This means that we don't see some things because our minds are focused on other things. Can you recall seeing an illustration of a chicken on page 61? If you did, well done: most people don't. Why not, because you didn't expect to see it? We only see what we expect to see, not what's there.

To sum up, we have learned that healthy relationships need good supplies of willpower, accurate thinking and self-control. These three ingredients for a happy relationship are seldom mentioned in marriage self-help books, yet they are crucial to making your conjugal lives a success.

Remember, what you think and believe about a situation is not always accurate. Try to see the issue or argument from your partner's perspective and give each other the time you both need to process what you are feeling. Never dismiss those feelings as trite or irrelevant; for most of us, feelings are all we have to guide us in our daily lives, especially when we are too tired or stressed to think clearly.

# 10

# MUSINGS

Priming

Is Mass Good for Your Marriage?

Projections

## PRIMING

Priming is an unconscious form of human memory concerned with perceptual identification of words and objects. It refers to activating particular representations or associations in memory just before carrying out an action or task. For example, a person who sees the word 'yellow' will be slightly faster to recognize the word 'banana'. This happens because yellow and banana are closely associated in memory. Additionally, priming can also refer to a technique in psychology used to train a person's memory in both positive and negative ways (www.psychologytoday.com).

The importance of priming for seduction was beautifully demonstrated by Will Smith's character Nicky in the film *Focus*. In an attempt to seduce the female character, Jess, played by Margot Robbie, Nicky used a cunning ploy known as priming to win her over. He used information about her preferences in men to create subtle clues all around her that reminded her of him. He pushed her buttons to such an extent that she experienced a surge of dopamine right before she saw him again, and she linked this feeling with how she felt about him.

'Priming' is the term used for how the brain forms associations based on the context of its environment. For example, finish this word: S_ _ _R.

What did you choose? Was it SOLAR or SUGAR, or some other word? Given that the last chapter mentioned food a few times and I even said 'sugar' explicitly, it wouldn't be surprising if you chose the word sugar. But could this affect your behaviour for the next few minutes? Perhaps if you had access to sweets or cake you might find yourself thinking about treating yourself. (You may be doing that right now, if so please remember to keep reading when you have finished eating.)

Priming can affect us more than we realise. Social psychologist John Bargh and his associates performed a famous experiment at New York University. He asked students to assemble a set of four-word sentences from a set of five words. For one half of the group, the scrambled sentences contained words such as *Florida, forgetful, gray, wrinkle* and *bald*. When they were finished they were sent down the hall to another room for a second experiment. The speed of their walk to the next room was really what Bargh was measuring. What do you think he discovered? The students that had been primed with words related to old age walked more slowly than the other group. They had no conscious awareness of this and none reported any change in their normal walking tempo when questioned.

Similar tests on African-American students found that merely naming their race on the application page of the test affected their scores. They scored worse in these tests than on tests where race was not mentioned. Women do poorly at maths when they are asked to name their gender on the test compared to when they don't have to, but interestingly, Asian women score better at maths when they are allowed to name their race. This is due to the widely held belief that Asian people are better at maths than other races.

Derren Brown, the psychological illusionist, is an expert at priming. He once took a duo of marketing executives on a bus tour of London and after an hour they met him back in his office. There he gave them a simple task to complete: create a poster for a new business idea, any idea that came to them. They set to work. Thirty minutes later he reappeared, full of smiles and nods as always. (Have you worked out why Derren nods all the time?) Before revealing their poster to him, he asked them would they mind if he tried to guess what they had drawn. They looked bemused but he set to work regardless. After five minutes he produced a rough sketch of a new business plan for a pet cemetery, with heavenly gates and featuring some wings and a drawing of a cuddly teddy bear. They were amazed when they revealed their poster. It was almost identical to his.

He then played a video montage of their bus journey. Along the route they took, he had positioned a number of billboards, advertising displays and people dressed in teddy-bear costumes. They had no conscious awareness that they had seen these prompts. Their memories could not recall the hints he had left for them, but their unconscious brains, their System 1s, had remembered and utilised each and every one.

We all have the ability to prime our partners, every day, if we so choose. If we direct our partner's attention to messages that are positive, life-enriching and satisfying, we will probably end up with happier spouses. But if the first thing you both do when you come in from work is watch the news, you are both already primed for negativity. If after the news you watch your favourite soap opera (which always has couples in crisis or in various stages of conflict), you are further priming yourself to notice problems in your own relationship. Many of the reality shows we watch also have an undercurrent of negativity in them, so if you watch TV together, try to find inspirational shows about how amazing people can be. (Good luck with that search.)

Scrolling through Facebook is just as dangerous for your relationship. It's filled with people showing off how happy they are with their latest purchase of a car or handbag, or yet another photograph of legs beside an exotic swimming pool (and there's always someone showing off their six-pack).

Envy and *Schadenfreude* are two emotions that are connected to the fortune or luck of others. They are evoked when we compare ourselves socially. Envy represents displeasure in others' fortunes, and sees an increase in the activity of the anterior cingulate cortex, or inner Sherlock, and shows less activity in the reward centre of the brain. *Schadenfreude* represents the pleasure in others' misfortune, and this shows up as a reduction in activity in the empathy areas of the brain, namely the full-length mirror.

Envy is very real, and if we allow ourselves to compare our relationship to others, be they celebrities or just friends, we will be primed to feel less satisfied with our own lives than if we maintain a state of gratitude. One leads to pessimism, the other leads to optimism. If you want to prime your relationship for success, read positive books (like this one) with life-affirming messages and surround yourself with positive people: they have more of an influence on you than you may realise.

## Is Mass Good for Your Marriage?

Researchers have discovered that sitting on hard wooden furniture promotes rigid thinking. They have also studied the impact of black uniforms on how people accept authority without question – think bouncers or door staff. As we have seen, reading statements about race, colour or gender can create changes in the brain that lead us to dismiss our own value as human beings. So putting all this together, is Mass good for your relationship? Well, most churches have hard wooden furniture and the priest wears black, not a good start.

I recently counted the word 'sin' or 'sinners' being used at least 25 times at an Irish Sunday Mass. In other words, I was being primed to feel ashamed of myself. If I feel ashamed of myself after Mass, will this help me relate better to my partner? Is shame a positive or a negative arousal chemical?

We know that shame releases cortisol and this creates a feeling of stress or discomfort. In my opinion, feeling ashamed is not going to make my relationship stronger. This would imply that going to Mass is *not* good for my relationship. I don't recall Jesus telling people they were sinners 25 times in just 30 minutes. I must have missed that bit.

## Projections

A number of years ago I was asked to be the relationship expert on the BBC TV show *You're Not the Man I Married*. One of the couples I worked with had a problem with romance. The wife, Marian, complained that her husband, Norman, wasn't romantic or spontaneous enough. My task was to help him become more romantic.

When I interviewed him, Norman admitted that nothing he did was ever good enough for Marian. So he no longer bothered. His confidence at organising day trips or evenings out for them both was non-existent. He confessed that the last time he managed to do something nice, Marian spent the entire time complaining that it wasn't what she wanted.

So I organised the following challenge for him. I took him to a children's play centre where he had to organise and host a party for the local children's drama group, about 17 children in total with ages ranging from 9 to 12. He was given a small budget and sent off shopping for games and food. He did really well; he even organised a bouncy castle.

At 2 o'clock on a damp Saturday afternoon, 20 children arrived for their party; three more than he had catered for. Before they went into the hall, the kids were taken to one side and given the following instructions by the production team – do your best to complain about everything that Norman does. The drinks won't be cold enough and the food won't be hot enough. 'Go to town on him,' we instructed. The drama kings and queens duly obliged. Poor Norman didn't know what hit him. There he was with 20 children running around, going crazy, food fights breaking out everywhere. It was total chaos.

But we weren't finished yet. One of the crew took Norman outside the hall for the mid-point interview. 'How are you getting on? How is it going?' he asked. While Norman was busy composing himself for the camera, the rest of the crew were sabotaging the bouncy castle. We took out the air stop at the back and slowly but surely it started to deflate. When Norman arrived back, he faced 20 children whining about the loss of their castle.

Norman was amazing. He quickly found what the problem was, kept his cool, and within minutes had the castle back to full inflation. The kids thought he was a hero. They all rallied around him and began cooperating with everything he asked of them. From that point on, the party was a huge success.

After it was all over, we again took Norman outside, and told him about our attempt to sabotage the party. He laughed it off on camera and made light of it; he was raging inside but held his composure remarkably well on camera.

I then brought his wife to a quiet room in a plush hotel, where we chatted about Norman's competency as a husband. She said he was great around the house, was a super dad to their son and a hard worker. I showed her the footage of the children's party. I wanted to see her reaction. She laughed as she saw him struggling to cope but then felt proud that he managed to turn it around so well. I wanted to know what her final thoughts were on the issue of romance and spontaneity. If he was clearly a competent husband and clearly well able to plan, organise and execute, where was the problem? Marian couldn't answer me.

In my opinion, the problem lay with Marian, not with Norman. It seemed to me that the reason she was so judgemental of him was nothing to do with romance. This was just a smokescreen for a deeper problem. I wondered if Marian was happy with herself. My overall impression was that she may have been projecting dissatisfaction onto Norman, as this deflected the attention away from herself. Norman never had a chance to feel dissatisfied, because he was so busy trying to make Marian happy.

Norman admitted later that day that his confidence was shot but he desperately wanted to protect Marian from ever having to change. I wondered with him if this was feasible, could he protect her forever, and what was the cost to him in doing so?

We are all like Marian in some ways. It's always easier to point the finger of blame at someone else rather than admit the problem is with us. Change like this isn't easy, and it takes buckets of courage to keep our marriages on track. What I learned from Marian and Norman was that no matter how hard someone tries to make their partner happy, it's up to each individual to take responsibility for their own happiness. No one can *make* you happy, that's *your* job.

## COMMUNICATION

Did you figure out why Derren Brown nods when he's speaking? Derren nods because he is priming us to agree with him. The nod is a gesture that we associate with the word 'Yes' (unless you are from India where you need to move your head from side to side.) Our System 1s notice his nodding gestures, and interprets them as a direction to agree with Derren. So this is what we do. It's a beautiful example of using unconscious body language to change our perception.

One of the casualties of the Internet revolution has been our ability to read body language. The simple fact is that when couples sit down together after a hard day's work, usually one of them is on a tablet or laptop and the other is watching television. Some couples sit in the same room watching different programmes, using headphones. Even watching the same movie together is not immune from the tech invasion. Usually one person is scrolling on their smartphone during the movie, chatting to friends or liking posts on Facebook. We have stopped complaining about this; we now accept it as the norm. I notice that couples seldom spend time looking at each other directly and not some form of a screen or electrical device.

To counter this, I give couples that very challenge: turn towards each other and gaze into each other's eyes. How do you think people react? Massive groans of awkwardness and displeasure. Once they do it, of course, they realise their spouse isn't that hard to look at after all.

Desmond Morris is the expert on reading body language. His book *People Watching: The Desmond Morris Guide to Body Language* is a must-have for anyone fascinated by how we communicate non-verbally. By learning this ancient form of communication, we can dramatically improve how we perceive others and how they perceive us. We will be more in tune with their moods and their feelings. The only sacrifice we have to make will be turning off our Wi-Fi and looking at our partners. Morris states most aptly that 'many technological advances are geared to the reduction of the stress, pollution and discomfort caused by ... technological advances' (Morris, p. 10). He also makes the interesting point that when it comes to what we tend to watch on TV, 'mostly we watch simulations of the quarrels, love affairs, parental devotion, and other age-old action – patterns just mentioned'. In other words, we watch on TV what we should be doing ourselves.

He speaks about two core sets of body-language facets that we need to understand: actions and gestures. Some actions are 'in-born': 'Essentially the idea is that the brain is programmed, rather like a computer, to link particular reactions with particular stimuli.' (*ibid.*, p. 4). Think of the newborn baby's immediate urge to suckle its mother's nipple. Other actions such as smiling and frowning are also in-born.

The range of gestures we have at our disposal is vast. There are parental signals, infantile signals and sexual signals, to name but a few. 'A gesture is any action that sends a visual signal to an onlooker. To become a gesture, an act has to be seen by someone else and has to communicate some piece of information to them' (*ibid.*, p. 21).

Gregory Bateson, the famous anthropologist, once said, 'The map is not the territory.' The most important aspect of a gesture is not the message we are trying to convey but the message that is being interpreted by the receiver. We sometimes have no control over this. In relationships that are going along smoothly, couples don't need to worry about interpreting their partner's body language accurately all the time. Each can make allowances for the other's errors, should they occur. Not so when there is conflict.

Mandy and Errol were together about seven years when they came to see me. From the moment they sat down, they turned away from each other. In my office I have funky red chairs that swivel, the type of chair you might see in a boutique hotel. Besides their pleasing style and shape, they also allow me to assess what's happening in the relationship before anyone even speaks. Couples in a good space swivel towards each other. Couples who are arguing tend to rotate away, as you would expect.

When someone is speaking to me about their relationship I am trying to monitor their partner's reactions to what they are saying at the same time. In this case, every time Mandy spoke, Errol raised his eyes to heaven, huffed and puffed, or looked down at the ground, and ended his reaction with a slight curl of his lips, also called a sneer.

John Gottman uses a more advanced system with his clients than just simple observation. He records each session and requests that the couple speak for 15 minutes about the issue in hand. He then analyses their body language with a system called SPAFF – the Specific Aspect Coding System. Through years of rigorous research he is now able to predict, with 90 per cent accuracy, which couples will divorce within five years. He watches out for sneers, hostile humour and other expressions of contempt. However, one of my clients I had mentioned this to pointed out that if Gottman makes this prediction and informs his couples that they are likely to divorce, their belief in his expertise may bring this to pass, in a form of self-fulfilling prophecy.

Emotions such as contempt tend to register on our faces even if we are not aware of them. The outward display of this emotion may be so fleeting that no one notices it, not even you. This is why Gottman records every session on video and has a team of trained observers with him in his 'Love Lab', lest he miss something himself.

According to Paul Ekman, the American psychologist, it's physically impossible to consciously control the five thousand muscles in your face. So if your partner says something that you don't agree with – let's say you are at a dinner party and your beloved expresses a racist sentiment that catches you by surprise – without being able to censor your face quickly enough, a close observer will notice your eyebrows being raised in a gesture of disbelief or shock.

Emotions like disbelief come and go. They begin in our System 1s but quickly make themselves known in our System 2s. According to Antony Damasio, the neuroscientist, 'most if not all emotional responses are the result of a long history of evolutionary fine tuning. Emotions are part of the bioregulatory devices with which we come equipped to survive' (Damasio, p. 53). So there you have it: you 'feel' in order to stay alive.

Emotions allow us to interpret the relative safety of our environment and our relationships and point us towards safety. Where we sometimes go astray is in letting our emotions interfere completely with rational thought. It is often more sagacious to *think* before acting on our feelings. Gmail helped millions of people manage this process better in 2015 by introducing the option of 'un-sending' that inappropriate email to their boss. What a handy tool!

## Is Praise Good for Your Relationship?

We might not think it, but giving each other praise regularly is essential to maintaining a happy and healthy brain. In a 2013 study, Tristen Inagaki and Naomi Eisenberger measured how subjects' brains responded to receiving praise from family and friends. They contacted the family and friends of each candidate and had them write letters about the individual in question. They were asked to write two types of letters: one was unemotional statements of fact – 'John has brown hair' – but in the other, they could express positive sentiments about the person.

The test subjects had their brains scanned as the two types of letters were read out. When the first type of letter was read out, there was little or no reaction in the brain, but when the positive statements were read out, there was a reaction in the ventral striatum or reward centre. It seems that saying nice things to one another activates the brain the same way as receiving a piece of cake, but in this case it has zero calories and is therefore guilt-free.

## How Can You Tell if Your Partner Is Lying?

Joe Navarro is a handsome, well-built ex-cop who was approached by the FBI to work with them as a special agent when he was just 23. Joe jumped at the chance and became one of the FBI's most important assets. Joe became an expert in reading non-verbal gestures, or body language to you and me. His work was made famous in the TV show *Lie To Me*.

In Navarro's excellent book *What Every Body Is Saying: An Ex-FBI Agent's Guide to Speed-Reading People*, we learn that approximately 80 per cent of what we communicate to others is in our body language, and about 37 per cent of the meaning of our words comes from the tone of voice we use.

So does this mean that we can tell when our partner is lying to us? Well, sort of. Joe believes that deception is one of the hardest aspects of body language to spot in others – remember, people have been lying since they were able to speak. Working with Joe, the FBI released a report in 2003 called 'A four domain model of Detecting Deception: An Alternative Paradigm for Interviewing'. In this report Joe expounded the idea that deceit could be detected through what he called 'limbic arousal'. What he found was that when we are telling the truth, we are able to display more empathic behaviours than when we are lying.

When people lie, they experience cognitive overload, which shows up in muscular stress. When people are lying to us they tend not to mirror us as there is a sense of discomfort in being around us. Your gorilla has been trained to spot this from your earliest days on the planet, so use him wisely. To expose lies, have the person sit opposite you with nothing in between you both, then, as they speak, watch what they do with their lower body. If they try to wrap their feet behind the table legs, for example, this might not be a good sign. Trust your instincts, always.

> ### Handy Hint from Brain Science
> To avoid escalating a conflict, grab a soft, comfy chair. Sitting down relaxes the body, which then sends messages to your brain to slow your breathing and reduce your heart rate. It's more difficult to stay angry when both of you are physically comfortable.

## CAN SMARTPHONES MAKE YOU CHEAT?

Eighty-five per cent of Americans check their smartphones within 15 minutes of waking up. One in three would prefer to give up sex rather than lose access to their smartphones.

Did you ever wonder why so many people are addicted to their smartphones? Is it the endless array of apps that we can download? Or the shiny screens with their millions of pixels? Perhaps it's addictive games like *Candy Crush* or *Farmville*?

When I ran my first marriage seminar in 2007, no one had a smartphone. At lunchtime couples would eat their food then chat together for the remainder of the time, usually with the other attendees.

Fast-forward to 2015: *everyone* has a smartphone, and at lunchtime the vast majority of couples don't communicate with anyone else, not even their future spouses. So how have smartphones got us hooked and, more importantly, could they cause us to cheat?

For most of his career, Nir Eyal worked in the video-gaming and advertising industries, where he learned the techniques that are used to motivate and manipulate users. Eyal put his vast experience and insider knowledge on the line by revealing the secret to why smartphones, apps and games are so addictive.

Smartphones are addictive in the same way that gambling and online gaming are addictive. There are four stages to the addiction. These are: 1. the Trigger, 2. the Action, 3. the Investment and 4. the Variable Reward. A trigger is a message that tells the user what to do next. When you see an advert for Coca-Cola, the trigger is the slogan: 'Drink Coke'. This is an external trigger. An internal trigger is the creation of an emotional state such as envy, pain, or the need for reward.

The action is the purchasing of the can of Coke. The investment is the belief that having bought the Coke and drank it, you are no longer thirsty. This embeds the idea in your brain that 'When I'm thirsty, I drink Coke'. This information is encoded in the basal ganglia. However, the brain likes novelty and while Coke contains caffeine, which is addictive, smartphones have no such properties. The key to their addiction is in what's called 'variable reward'.

When you check your email, you may have a nice, loving email from a partner waiting in your inbox to cheer you up. You might also have a bill from your mobile-phone provider. A customer may have left you a glowing testimonial or a colleague may have undermined you in a group email. You just never know what you are going to get. The anticipation you feel *before* you check your email releases dopamine. This disappears if all you find are phone bills. This is what's known as 'variable reward' and the entire process has us addicted to our smartphones.

So can smartphones cause us to cheat? Well, they certainly give us the tools to cheat. Being able to access websites such as the Ashley Madison website, which was hacked in 2015, directly from your mobile, increases the likelihood of cheating if only because of the availability factor. But my concern is that by rewiring our brains to need constant dopamine hits from apps or emails or shopping sites, we are, in effect, making it more likely that we will feel less satiated from mere contact with our beloved. Just sitting in their company doesn't seem sufficient any more. We seem to 'need' to be online, too. Some of us seem to crave attention from others, outside our relationships. Is this healthy? Where will it end? Three years ago, a couple I worked with told me they wished each other sweet dreams on Facebook, while lying beside each other in bed. I thought they were crazy. Three years on, it no longer sounds that odd.

## WHY DO SOME PEOPLE CHANGE SO MUCH AFTER MARRIAGE?

Just recently, one of the couples I had prepared for marriage paid me a visit. They were in trouble after only three months of marriage. Jennifer and Rogan were Canadians who had moved to Ireland four years ago when Jennifer's family had settled here. They seemed happy when I met them for their marriage course and I didn't foresee any problems, so I was a bit taken aback when they arrived at my office.

Jennifer started the session bemoaning the fact that Rogan didn't seem interested in making her happy. I wondered what she meant. Some of the conversation went as follows:

> Jennifer: Ever since we got married, Rogan goes about his business like he did before we married. He has kept the exact same routine: he goes to work, comes home, eats dinner, reads his books, checks the sports results and goes to bed.
> Me: Was this the same routine he had before you got married?
> J: Yes, exactly the same.
> Me: So why did you think it would change after marriage, Jennifer, and how do you want Rogan's routine to be different going forward?
> J: Because I'm his wife now, and he's my husband so he should put *me* first. He should come home from work and make sure that I'm happy, that I'm not bored, and he should be more romantic.

At this point, I asked Jennifer where she got her job description of the role of 'husband' from.

After a long pause, she admitted that her ideas came from romance novels that she had read voraciously in her late teens and even in college. She had never checked if these romantic ideals were even remotely grounded in reality. It wasn't until she had a husband that she could gain awareness of the unconscious expectations she had of Rogan. We spent the remainder of the session exploring what was realistic and unrealistic. Jennifer had fallen for a classic stereotype of husbandry, the rescuer Prince Charming stereotype.

Couples will frequently assume the roles and responsibilities in marriage that they observed in their parents' own marriages. So if Dad was great at DIY and mended everything in the house, some women assume that their husbands should be just as proficient as their fathers, leading to great disappointment in some households.

A useful exercise as a couple is to write a list of the common household chores you face each month and write down who you think did these chores in your family of origin. My guess is that unconsciously you may expect your own husband or wife to do the same type of chores, from paying bills to picking the children up from school. Unless couples can negotiate around this list effectively, they may be in line for a good deal of resentment.

## STEREOTYPES

Another reason some people change personality after marriage is due to the powerful influence of stereotypes. A stereotype is a set of beliefs or characteristics we hold about someone based on their race, gender, nationality or age. Usually they're not true. For example, African-American men are likely to be gangsters, lack intelligence and are prone to sporadic bouts of violence. Women are bad at maths, bad at driving, not that logical and prone to irrationality. Teenagers are self-centred vandals who love to break the rules and take drugs. Old people are bitter, lazy and useless to society. Chinese people lack a sense of humour. Russians can't be trusted. The Irish are alcoholics and the British are imperialistic. The French are arrogant and rude while the Germans are cold but incredibly efficient.

None of these are true, they are all stereotypes.

Now let me ask you this question. Which of the following words do you associate with the word 'husband' and which do you associate with the word 'wife'? List these words in two columns, under the headings 'Husband' and 'Wife'.

Strong  Dependable  Adorable  Artistic  Loving  Kind
Meek  Vulnerable  Agreeable  Domestic  Organised
Sheltered  Romantic  Provider  Nurturer  Carer  Aggressor
Violent  Controlling  Powerful  Possessive  Stubborn
Delightful  Altruistic  Engaging  Sexy  Provocative  Shy
Cowardly  Tough  Hardy  Funny  Sociable  Engaging
Manipulative  Spiteful  Thoughtful  Romantic  Sinister

Did you notice a pattern? Did you unconsciously ascribe certain traits to husbands but not to wives and vice versa? Why did you do this? Where did you get these ideas from? Stereotypes can harm our relationships. When we judge our partner with a stereotype, we prevent them from ever being fully authentic and we pigeonhole ourselves in a negative way.

## THE 'MARITAL ENSNAREMENT EFFECT'

Many couples who get married feel trapped by the process. Having been together for ten years or so, they get married because society expects them to, not because they see any intrinsic benefits in doing so. In fact, one of the hardest questions for engaged couples to answer is 'Why do you want to get married?' Lots of people get married so they can have a big day out, i.e. a wedding. This is not the wisest reason to get married. In Ireland, a marriage is a legally binding contract that removes a host of freedoms from the couple. If they want to separate in the future, they may have to pay maintenance to one another, which can come as a shock to many people.

The experience of feeling trapped within a marriage can cause people to behave in strange ways. They may try to sabotage the marriage by gaining weight, going off sex, being nasty or even becoming physically abusive. I call this range of behaviours the 'marital ensnarement effect'. In my opinion, once a couple feels that they don't want to be married to one another, and where all other avenues have been explored, including marital therapy, then at this point they should be helped to separate. Hundreds of my clients reported growing up in families that were constantly at war thanks to the marital ensnarement effect. The consequences for my clients were severe depression and low self-esteem, even bulimia and anorexia in some cases. We may believe that once two people get married, whether they are happy or not, they should stay together for better or worse. I can't say I agree with this philosophy.

## PHILIP GEORGE ZIMBARDO

In 1971, Philip George Zimbardo, using a grant from the US Office of Naval Research, began the study in which 24 clinically sane individuals from 'good' backgrounds, and from various different careers, were randomly assigned to be 'prisoners' or 'guards' in a mock dungeon located in the basement of the psychology building at Stanford University. Unfortunately, the planned two-week study into the psychology of prison life had to be shut down after only six days, due to the emotional trauma experienced by the participants. The subjects quickly began acting out their roles, with 'guards' becoming sadistic and 'prisoners' showing extreme passivity and depression. The guards invented cruel punishments regularly for their prisoners. Remember, the prisoners had committed no crimes. The prison guards knew these men were innocent and were merely subjects in an experiment, just like them.

The prisoners rioted on the second day. The guards retaliated, stripping them naked and punishing them with physical exercise. One prisoner even went on hunger strike: all this just a few days into the experiment.

So what did Zimbardo conclude from his dramatic research project? Dr Zimbardo has written in *The Lucifer Effect: Understanding How Good People Turn Evil* that 'good people can be induced, seduced, and initiated into behaving in evil ways. They can also be led to act in irrational, stupid, self-destructive, antisocial, and mindless ways when they are immersed in "total situations" that impact human nature in ways that challenge our sense of the stability and consistency of individual personality, of character, and of morality' (Zimbardo, p. 221).

In my professional opinion, some people should never get married. People with malfunctioning brains are most at risk of behaving just like Zimbardo's prison wardens. For them, the 'total situation' that Zimbardo refers to is marriage. It's simply too much stress for them to cope with. The need to think about the other, to intuit what their husband or wife is thinking; to support them and do all that marriage involves, is just too much. Their brains can't cope. They become aggressive and violent as a result. I really think that pre-marriage courses should be mandatory, not just because it's my business, but because I have to work with the damaged children of the violent, the alcoholic, and the abusing parents who are unable to care for their children.

If people were encouraged to think more carefully about the consequences of having children and the reality of being parents it might save a good deal of heartbreak for all concerned. Hard to implement, I know, but worth thinking about.

## HOW TO GET YOUR PARTNER TO CHANGE

William Greenough was a professor at the University of Illinois until his death in 2014. One of his associates at the university, Neal J. Cohen, said of Bill that 'his research revealed that environment, exercise and training continued to shape the brain throughout the lifespan' (Cohen, see https://news.illinois.edu/news/14/0108obit_williamgreenough.html). Bill performed a famous experiment on lab rats where he compared the impact of a stimulating environment on the size of the rats' brains, compared to other rats that were left alone in cages with no stimulus. He discovered that those rats that had stimulation increased brain size significantly compared to their fellow unstimulated rats. In other words, we can continually grow our brains in different ways once the environment and our life's context are in alignment with this goal.

This means we are all capable of change. But can you facilitate change in someone else? It turns out you can.

In *Switch: How To Change Things When Change Is Hard*, Chip and Dan Heath created the following master plan to facilitate change in others. You can use this strategy to make him do more housework or make her more romantic, anything you like, really, once you follow the steps.

Step 1. Make the person feel the need for change. This has to happen at an emotional and not just an intellectual level.
Step 2. Be very specific about what it is you want them to change.
Step 3. Point them to the bright spots, i.e. teach them how to be optimistic with regard to the change.

This simple plan can be used by you to make any changes you want in your life or to direct anyone else to make the changes *they* want to make. The key is they must *want* to make the changes, too. Change can't be imposed on them.

Gorillas like to be the 'King of the Jungle' but when it comes to making changes, as you have seen, you need to put your professor firmly in control.

## CONCLUSION

Wow, there you have it. We're finished. Thank you for accompanying me on this incredible journey. I hope that you've enjoyed the experience of reading as much as I enjoyed the writing. You have been a wonderful companion to me as I wrote. If you are a teacher, an accountant, a nurse, or a therapist like me, I hope that what I've said here has some resonance for you.

And finally, to sum up this book in just one sentence, remember the words of hypnotherapist Milton Erickson: 'Trust your unconscious, it knows more than you do.'

# Afterword

To show my gratitude for purchasing and reading this book, I would like to give you some discounts for my brain-science programmes. On www.loverewired.com you will find a range of programmes to help you succeed in life. Just use the coupon code '50% OFF' for any that you like and you will receive a discount for each programme.

Please feel free to get in touch with me, tell me a little bit about yourself, are you single, married, or a parent, or maybe you're looking for love? If so, email me at info@loverewired.com; I would love to hear from you and help you any way I can.

Finally, the names and details of all my case studies have been changed to protect the identity of my clients, any similarities to people you may know is purely coincidental.

David Kavanagh, 2016

# Bibliography

## Books

Brann, A. (2015) *Neuroscience for Coaches: How To Use the Latest Insights for the Benefit of Your Clients*, London: Kogan Page.

Baumeister, R. and Tierney, J. (2011) *Willpower: Why Self-Control Is the Secret to Success*, London: Penguin Books.

Chabris, C. and Simons, D. (2010) *The Invisible Gorilla*, London: Harper Collins.

Cialdini, R. (2007) *Influence: The Psychology of Persuasion*, New York: Harper Collins.

Cozolino, L. (2006) *The Neuroscience of Human Relationships, Attachment and the Developing Social Brain*, New York: W.W. Norton.

Csikszentmihalyi, M. (2002) *Flow: The Psychology of Optimal Experience*, England: Rider.

Damasio, A. (1999) *The Feeling of What Happens: Body and Emotion in the Making of Consciousness*, Florida: Harcourt Press.

De Bono, E. (1990) *Lateral Thinking*, London: Penguin Books.

De Mello, A. (1990) *Awareness*, New York: Zondervan.

Dweck, C. (2006) *Mindset: How You Can Fulfil Your Potential*, London: Constable and Robinson.

Gardner, D. (2010) *Future Babble: How To Stop Worrying and Love the Unpredictable*, England: Random House.

Gerhardt, S. (2004) *Why Love Matters: How Affection Shapes your Baby's Brain*, East Sussex: Routledge.

Gladwell, M. (2008) *Outliers: The Story of Success*, London: Penguin Group.

Goldberg, E. (2009) *The New Executive Brain: Frontal Lobes in a Complex World*, New York: Oxford University Press.

Heath, C. and D. (2010) *Switch: How To Change Things When Change Is Hard*, London: Random House.

Kahneman, D. (2012) *Thinking Fast and Slow*, London: Penguin Books.

Miller, G.R. (1980) *Persuasion: New Directions in Theory and Research*, Beverly Hills: Sage.

Morris, D. (2002) *People Watching: The Desmond Morris Guide to Body Language*, London: Vintage.

Navarro, J. and Karlins, M. (2007) *What Every Body Is Saying: An Ex-FBI Agent's Guide to Speed-Reading People*, United States of America: Harper Collins.

Pillay, S. (2011) *Your Brain and Business*, United States of America: Pearson.

Stanovich, K. (2011) *Rationality and the Reflective Mind*, Great Britain: Oxford University Press.

Syed, M. (2011) *Bounce: The Myth of Talent and the Power of Practice*, Great Britain: Fourth Estate.

Toffler, A. (1971) *Future Shock*, Great Britain: Pan Books.

Zimbardo, P. (2008) *The Lucifer Effect: Understanding How Good People Turn Evil*, London: Ebury.

## ARTICLES

Hill, S.E. and Buss, D.M. (2008) 'The mere presence of opposite-sex others on judgments of sexual and romantic desirability: opposite effects for men and women', *Personality and Social Psychology Bulletin*, May, 34(5), 635–47, doi: 10.1177/014616720 7313728. Epub 2008 Feb 26.

Sharot, T., Riccardi, A.M., Raio, C.M. and Phelps, E.A. (2007) 'Neural Mechanisms Mediating Optimism Bias', *Nature*, 450 (7166), 102-5 PMID: 17960136.

Silani, G. (2014) 'Empathy for Social Exclusion Involves the Sensory-Discriminative Component of Pain: A Within-Subject fMRI Study', International School for Advanced Studies (SISSA) of Trieste, *Social Cognitive and Affective Neuroscience* (2014).


## RECOMMENDED READING

Amen, D. (2008) *Magnificent Mind at Any Age*, New York: Crown Publishing.

Bernays, E. (1928) *Propaganda*, USA: Ig Publishing.

Canfield, J. (2005) *The Success Principles: How To Get From Where You Are To Where You Want To Be*, London: Harper Collins.

Chomsky, N. (1991) *Media Control: The Spectacular Achievements of Propaganda*, New York: Seven Stories Press.

Cox, T. (2003) *Superflirt*, London: Dorling Kindersley.

Dooley, R. (2012) *Brainfluence: 100 Ways to Persuade and Convince Consumers with Neuromarketing*, New Jersey: Wiley.

Eagleman, D. (2011) *Incognito: The Secret Lives of the Brain*, Edinburgh: Canongate Books.

Eyal, N. (2014) *Hooked: How To Build Habit-Forming Products*, New York: Penguin Books.

Fisher, H. (2004) *Why We Love: The Nature and Chemistry of Romantic Love*, New York: Owl Books.

Gibb, B.J. (2007) *The Rough Guide to the Brain*, London: Penguin Books.

Gladwell, M. (2005) *Blink: The Power of Thinking Without Thinking*, London: Penguin Books.

Goleman, D. (1996) *Emotional Intelligence: Why It Can Matter More Than IQ*, New York: Bloomsbury.

James, O. (2010) *How Not to F\*\*\* Them Up*, London: Vermilion.

Kabat-Zinn, J. (1994) *Wherever You Go, There You Are*, London: Piatkus.

LeDoux, J. (2002) *Synaptic Self: How Our Brains Become Who We Are*, New York: Penguin Books.

# Bibliography

Lieberman, M. (2013) *Social: Why Our Brains Are Wired To Connect*, New York: Broadway Books.

Lynch, Z. and Laursen, B. (2009) *The Neuro Revolution: How Brain Science Is Changing Our World,* New York: St. Martin's Press.

McTaggart, L. (2007) *The Intention Experiment: Use Your Thoughts To Change The World*, London: Harper Collins.

Medina, J. (2014) *Brain Rules: 12 Principles for Surviving and Thriving at Work, Home and School*, Seattle: Pear Press.

Medina, J. (2014) *Brain Rules For Baby: How To Raise a Smart and Happy Child From Zero To Five*, Seattle: Pear Press.

Ranan, D. (2006) *Double Cross: The Code of the Catholic Church*, London: Theo Press.

Thaler, R.H. and Sunstein, C.R. (2009) *Nudge: Improving Decisions about Health, Wealth and Happiness*, London: Penguin Books.